Domestic abuse is among the issues facing the church feel unprepared to address all the complexities related to such a difficult topic. I thank God that Greg Wilson and Jeremy Pierre have made that difficult task a little easier by offering the Church a biblical resource designed to help you help others. *When Home Hurts* is the theologically rich, field tested approach to domestic abuse intervention that the Church needs today.

Chris Moles
Author of *The Heart of Domestic Abuse; Gospel Solutions for Men Who Use Violence and Control in the Home*

Greg Wilson and Jeremy Pierre have written an exceptional book that should be required reading for pastors, counselors, and ministry leaders in the Church. Comprehensive in its scope and compassionate in its approach, I have no doubt that we will be returning to this resource time and time again to offer competent, biblical, gracious counsel to the abused. Wilson and Pierre bring a level of theological clarity on the topic of abuse that is both compelling and convincing. With their help your hearts and minds will be equipped to offer solid and informed counsel as well as grounding your trust, hope, and faith in our merciful and compassionate Savior. I cannot commend this book more heartily.

Jonathan D. Holmes
Executive Director, Fieldstone Counseling
Author of *Counsel for Couples: A Biblical and Practical Guide for Marriage Counseling*

When Home Hurts is packed with clarifying biblical insights and concrete action steps for church leaders who encounter domestic abuse. Tremendous wisdom and experience have gone into the shepherding plans and assessment tools found in this book. This makes it an essential and invaluable guide that every church should have at the ready.

Darby Strickland
Author of *Is it Abuse? A Biblical Guide to Identifying Domestic Abuse and Helping Victims*
Faculty member, CCEF

When Home Hurts is an exemplary resource in equipping the Church on how to rightly and wisely respond to domestic abuse. Guided by the Word of God and accurately informed by research and experts, every page provides instructive hands-on help for church leaders, counselors, or concerned friends and family. There may not be a resource more desperately needed in the Church than this book. Without hesitation I recommend it as a foremost resource for anyone seeking to help someone who is trapped under the weight of an abusive relationship.

Eliza Huie
LCPC and Dean of Biblical Counseling at Metro Baltimore Seminary
Author of *Raising Kids in a Screen-Saturated World, Raising Teens in a Sex-Saturated World,*
and *The Whole Life: 52 Weeks of Biblical Self-Care*

An excellent treatment of one of the most challenging topics facing the church today. Pierre and Wilson have tackled abuse in a way that is both practical and theologically robust. Church leaders and counselors will want to read this now to gain a better understanding of abuse from several important perspectives, but then have it stored on a handy bookshelf for the sad day you need its contents in a time of crisis in the life of someone you love and shepherd.

Steve Viars
Faith Church and Biblical Counseling Ministries

There is a great need for more Christian resources on abuse which understand that safety is the primary concern when a victim has the courage to confide their experience of abuse. That is why I am grateful for *When Home Hurts*. My advice, read it before you need it. The 'fog of war' around an abuse scenario is dense. Confusion abounds. Gain an understanding of your guiding priorities before the wellbeing of a spouse and children are at stake based on your pastoral response. You will be glad you did.

Brad Hambrick
Pastor of Counseling, The Summit Church, Durham,
North Carolina

This book will be a game changer for churches who want to handle situations of domestic abuse with Biblical wisdom, compassion and practical helps. I loved how the authors laid out so clearly God's overarching plan for relationships, including marriage. Abuse, harshness, and using one's strength, authority, or power to tear others down diminishes their God given capabilities, demeans their dignity, and destroys their capacity for choice. Pastors will love the theological nuance and practical ways the authors lay out how to have tough conversations with victims, abusers and congregants. Counselors will appreciate the prioritizing of safety planning and trauma work with victims as well as the fresh insights of how to handle the passive resistance of the abuser.

Leslie Vernick
International speaker, relationship coach and author of 7 books
including *The Emotionally Destructive Relationship* and *The Emotionally Destructive Marriage*

An accessible and practical handbook for the church and her people. *When Home Hurts* is written with care, attention to even the most minute detail, and a dedication to seeing the whole body built up and flourishing. A needed work for these times.

Lore Ferguson Wilbert
Author of *Handle With Care: How Jesus Redeems the Power of Touch in Life and Ministry*

Domestic abuse is a complex and heavy burden for all who are involved and aware of the situation. The sad reality is that this burden is widespread both outside the church and within it. As a church leader, you will likely encounter people experiencing or impacted by domestic abuse. What will you do when that time comes? Pierre and Wilson bring years of wisdom from studying God's Word and applying it to hurting homes in order to help you bear the heavy burden of domestic abuse when it comes to your church. They offer a robust biblical investigation of the hearts of those involved and the harsh realities of abuse. *When Home Hurts* will help church leaders prepare themselves and their congregations with a deep biblical understanding of abuse and practical instruction on how to respond to it. This helpful resource will alleviate the concern and stress that will come in these difficult situations by helping define what your roles are and what they are not, giving you a plan and procedures to follow, and identifying key sources of support. I cannot recommend it higher.

Curtis W. Solomon
Executive Director, The Biblical Counseling Coalition

Abuse is happening more than we want and more than we know. Is your church prepared? From walking with both victim and oppressor, to setting up care teams and doing public communication wisely, *When Home Hurts* addresses every aspect of what a church needs to know to have a strong, merciful and deeply biblically balanced response to abuse. Written by wise and experienced church leaders, for church leaders, this book takes an extremely practical approach rooted in very clear and thoughtful theological categories. I am thrilled that this book finally exists!

J. Alasdair Groves
Executive Director, Christian Counseling and Educational
Foundation (CCEF)
Co-author of *Untangling Emotions*

No one sees, comprehends, and confronts abuse in relationships more clearly and wisely than the God who speaks through Scripture. This book will help you hear what He has to say. Few experiences of suffering appear more overwhelming and complex than domestic abuse. This book will equip you with relevant truths of the gospel so that you can respond with strength, peace, and simplicity. It will serve the church. It will serve all who intend to care well for those who abuse and those who suffer under abuse. I appreciate the careful work of Jeremy Pierre and Greg Wilson and commend this resource to you.

John Henderson
Associate Professor of Biblical Counseling,
The Southern Baptist Theological Seminary, Louisville, Kentucky

WHEN HOME HURTS

A GUIDE FOR RESPONDING WISELY
TO DOMESTIC ABUSE IN YOUR CHURCH

Jeremy Pierre & Greg Wilson

CHRISTIAN
FOCUS

Copyright © Jeremy Pierre & Greg Wilson 2021

paperback ISBN 978-1-5271-0722-9
ebook ISBN 978-1-5271-0819-6

10 9 8 7 6 5 4 3 2 1

Published in 2021
Reprinted in 2021
by
Christian Focus Publications Ltd,
Geanies House, Fearn, Ross-shire,
IV20 1TW, Scotland.

www.christianfocus.com

Cover design by Pete Barnsley

Printed in the USA

Contents

To my sister Wendy,
now safe.
JP

To Cristi and Sara,
for your unwavering support and love.
GW

Quick Reference Guide

Pressing Question	Where to Find an Answer
What is abuse? What does the Bible say about it?	Chapter 2, Section, 'Understanding Abuse Biblically,' page 39
How do I determine if someone is being abusive?	Chapter 3, Section, 'A Framework for Discerning Abuse Dynamics,' page 65
What if I think a person is just claiming victimhood?	Chapter 4, Introductory Section, page 81
What if I think she is making a false accusation?	Appendix A, 'FAQs on Domestic Abuse Care,' page 229. See also Chapter 1, Section 'Why Active Involvement is Difficult,' page 23
What if I think they're both being abusive?	Appendix A, 'FAQs on Domestic Abuse Care,' page 229
What if the husband is the victim, and the wife is the abuser?	Appendix F, 'When Wives Abuse Husbands,' page 275
How do I confront someone who's been accused of abuse?	Chapter 5, Section, 'What to Do When First Approaching an Abusive Spouse,' page 106

How do I help her discern if separation is warranted?	Chapter 4, Subsection, '7. Help her make a personal safety plan,' page 97
Is abuse a biblical reason for divorce?	Appendix B, 'FAQs on Separation, Divorce, and Reunification After Abuse,' page 237
Where can an abused spouse get logistical help?	Appendix C, 'National and State Domestic Violence Resources,' page 249

Acknowledgments

Willie MacKenzie gets credit for the existence of this resource. He kept after me for years about the importance of a resource for church leaders to address domestic abuse with biblical fidelity and practical wisdom. I knew I was not qualified to produce such a resource alone. So when I met Greg Wilson, I knew I'd found the missing piece to the project. His countless hours in the counseling room with both victims and abusers have developed in him eyes to discern the underlying dynamics that would be missed without such experience. Writing together was a joyful push-and-pull toward what we hope is a resource that's both faithful and insightful. In terms of those we learned from through talks and reading, Greg attempts to thank them all below. I second him on every one. Finally, I cannot say enough about my wife Sarah, who keeps our home a refuge from the storms of life.

—JP

JP, thank you for agreeing to supervise my D.Ed.Min. project at SBTS on domestic abuse care in the church that was the basis for this book. To those who have experienced hurt and pain in homes and relationships that should be safe, and trusted me with the stories that have helped inform this book, you are so courageous. Our prayer is that this book helps you and others see God's perspective on your experience, that homes and churches will be safer. Chris, Kirsten, Cache, Darby, and Joy, our monthly calls have sharpened me and kept me sane. Leslie, Matt, Josh, Brian, Lore, Summer, Trevor, Jeff, Linda, Angie, Beau, John, Jeremy, Jen and so many others have helped to hone and refine my thinking on this topic. My faithful assistant Mandy helped keep my counseling practice running smoothly during this project, and also helped us compile Appendix C. Cristi and Sara, you are both loved more than you know. Thank you for putting up with the nearly incessant clicking of my keyboard for the past several years.

—GW

We would both like to thank Willie MacKenzie and the team at Christian Focus Publications for sharing in our passion to provide help for homes that hurt due to domestic abuse. Thanks to Anne Norrie for editing the initial manuscript and to Rosanna Burton for putting up with our last-minute changes and revisions to the final manuscript. We also want to thank James Amour and his design team at Christian Focus for help with the cover design and the illustrations, and for letting us use that art at whenhomehurts.com as well.

Preface

We hadn't heard from my sister in two years. My family's first contact with her was an unexpected phone call from the guy she'd eloped with, letting us know she was in critical condition with a ruptured spleen. They'd been mountain biking, and my sister had fallen down a hill.

The spleen is a fist-sized organ in the abdomen that both filters blood and supplies life-giving cells that fight bacteria. It's a fairly delicate organ. When ruptured, the spleen can pour blood into the abdominal area sometimes requiring emergency surgery to keep someone alive. My sister was undergoing such a surgery.

The surgery was successful, and she recovered. Through that crisis, our family was able to re-establish our relationship with her, even after the unexplained years-long silence. But such things are forgotten in the joy of a baby girl arriving. Maybe that beautiful little girl was the key to making everything normal again.

At that point, no one knew the real cause of the spleen rupture. It was no hill that caused it, no mountain bike. It was something much smaller—something that was roughly the same size as the spleen it had ruptured. A fist. Or maybe a knee. It's hard to tell exactly. The details of that beating, and the many that came before and after, blend together for my sister in a haze of secrecy. And she would have remained in that gloom except for a realization that came to her suddenly one afternoon. Like sunlight cutting unexpectedly through thick clouds, my sister realized that the abuse she'd gradually adjusted to as normal would be the only normal her daughter would know.

That realization—and that realization alone—gave her the resolve to tell someone. Every other idea had been imperceptibly corrupted by this toxic normal. She had believed God wanted her to endure this suffering as a loyal wife. She had thought she was in too far to expect help from anyone else. She had wondered if this was just what real marriages were like, outside her idyllic upbringing. These thoughts were all corrupted. But that insight about her daughter, like sunlight from another sky, was one of the few ideas her abuse had not yet touched.

I won't describe the harrowing escape that happened the afternoon my sister decided to reach out. I'll only describe the responses she found when she did. When she called my mom, she unlocked the fierce courage latent in a modest woman. My sister described her home life, wondering how her disclosure would be received. My mom responded not in the form of sunlight, but of lightning: 'Wendy, who is your God? Is it God, or is it your husband?'

Sometimes God uses sunshine and sometimes He uses lightning to light up the soul. That truth about who God is affirmed all the right things and undermined all the wrong things in my sister's thinking. It gave her clarity to open up. And what she found was not only a mother and father willing to help set wrongs right, but a whole church full of people who loved her—and housed her, offered employment to her, and provided childcare for her, thereby assuring her of the Lord's tender care. Gradually, my sister came to find herself in a new normal, a different kind of home than the one that had hurt her.

This book is not about my sister. I've shared enough of her story, other than one last comment I can't help but make: She is safe, happy, and strong in the Lord. I write this preface with her blessing, because this book isn't for her. It is for the countless women who need the right people to respond the right way when these women find the courage to disclose that home hurts.

Greg and I wrote this book to help you be the kind of church leader, church member, friend, parent, sibling, or neighbor who responds wisely. We want the Church to be a new normal for those grown accustomed to abuse—a home that doesn't hurt those inside, but instead welcomes them into the tender care of the Lord.

JP

Section 1

How to Understand Abuse

You are probably reading this book because you want to help someone who may be suffering under domestic abuse, but you don't know how. You want to respond wisely, but you're not confident you understand enough to do so.

Understanding abuse and the people caught up in it are essential to wise response. In the three chapters that make up this section, we want to provide a framework for doing just that. We will give some key ideas about your role in the present situation, about the dynamics that make abuse different from other marital problems, and how each spouse experiences those dynamics. We hope this knowledge brings more confidence to take the right action.

But more than knowledge, what brings the most confidence is God's presence. We want you to be sure that God will be with you as you enter into this situation. We know it's not easy being a pastor, church leader, family member, or friend facing such a difficult situation. But rest assured, the Lord desires that we respond wisely, and He will supply the wisdom to do so. In fact, you get the privilege of displaying the heart of God—kind, stable, self-giving—to people who've had the opposite displayed to them. You get to be an agent of God's love for someone who may have forgotten what real love is—and what it looks like in the family of God.

1

Understanding Your Role as an Agent of God's Love

I swore never to be silent whenever and wherever human beings endure suffering and humiliation. We must always take sides. Neutrality always helps the oppressor, never the victim. Silence encourages the tormentor, never the tormented.
—Elie Wiesel Nobel Acceptance Speech, 1986

Rescue me, Lord, from evil men.
     Keep me safe from violent men.
(Ps. 140:1 CSB)

You may not know what it is to pray a prayer like this. You may never have cried out to God from behind a locked door, hugging your knees and wondering how much the rage on the other side will build up this time. But you're picking up this book in part because you want to know how to help someone who does have to pray this way. In fact, your reading this book may be the Lord's answer to her prayer.

Whether you are a pastor, a church leader, a friend, or a family member of someone you sense is under threat, you may feel paralyzed as to how you ought to respond to a situation you didn't cause, you don't know the full details of, and frankly scares you to death. But you also know paralysis is not an option when someone vulnerable is at risk.

Love is at the heart of God's will for you in this situation. Love, in fact, is at the heart of God's will for all of our relationships. It is the fulfillment of God's design for us, the realization of our greatest potential (Matt. 22:37-40; Rom. 13:8-10). But you may be surprised to learn that one of the primary tests of whether love is genuine is if it motivates a person to hate what is evil and to uphold what is good (Rom. 12:9-21). Love involves hate—a strong aversion to what harms others and dishonors the Lord. And it involves a strong attraction to what benefits others and honors the Lord. Love is the reverse of abuse because it builds others up at cost to self, rather than builds self up at cost to others. But love is not an equal opposite—it's far more powerful because, unlike abuse, love is sourced from the eternal depths of God's heart. You are an agent of a love much bigger than you. This love goes beyond sentiment, actually accomplishing good in someone else's life. It is dedication to their good. This is God's disposition toward people, and that should be a very encouraging thought for you as you try to help them. The love required to bring healing in this situation does not come from you. You are just an agent of God's love.

But how is love expressed in such an unclear and dangerous situation? In normal life, love often comes in pastels, the thousand gentle hues of human interaction. You enjoy light conversation, you overlook small offenses, you learn to appreciate people for who they are with all their shortcomings.

But when it comes to loving people in the swirling shadows of domestic abuse, love must come in stronger colors—colors that stand out in the gloom.

To the person being abused, your love comes in the color of dawn—a bright contrast to darkness, offering a new way of seeing life her eyes had forgotten. To the person committing abuse, your love is the color of alarm, disrupting the haze that hides his behaviors. To the family, friends, and church that surround them, your love is the color of the horizon, giving them a wider perspective to help them navigate this situation. In the dark grays of domestic abuse, your love comes best in stronger colors than normal.

We use the metaphor of strong colors to illustrate active care for those in an abusive relationship, as opposed to merely vague awareness of it. Our hope for this book is that the color of your love toward victims and abusers will represent the love that God has for them. Our goal is not just to call you as a church leader, friend, or family member to be involved, but to show you how to be involved in ways that reflect God's heart as displayed in His Word, and in ways that do not cause further harm.

Why Active Involvement Is Difficult

But you may still be hesitant about why it's necessary to be involved. That hesitation is certainly understandable in an unfamiliar and threatening situation like this. But let's get rid of that hesitation with some firm conviction since without solid conviction you'll lose heart in the process.

I am scared of making a mistake.
Let's put this to rest right away. You will not make *a* mistake. You will make many mistakes. The nature of hazy situations is that you will not immediately know what is best to do at any

given point. This is part of the process. Part of our job in this book is to provide a framework that will help you avoid the kind of mistakes that cause harm.

Fear of failure is often the greatest enemy of righteousness. Do not fear. There is a secret that will make your mistakes far less likely to harm anyone else: the virtue of humility. Humility—that is, both an awareness of your own limitations and a willingness to be corrected as you go—will keep you seeking the right knowledge for wise response, both from Scripture and from those suffering under abuse. Humility invites the grace of God (James 4:6; 1 Pet. 5:5).

I have no experience with these situations.
You may have little experience with domestic abuse situations, but you can still be a learner and a helper. You may not have chosen to be in this situation, but God in His mysterious providence has placed you in it to help someone who is hurting.

You are also seeking wisdom from people who do have experience with these situations. We hope this book can be a helpful initial guide, but we also commend resources produced by other people with experience and specific training in domestic violence, trauma, victim advocacy, abuser intervention, and related subjects. You should also get to know the folks involved in local domestic violence shelters, victim advocates, batterer intervention programs, and knowledgeable legal experts. We will say more about a coordinated community response in the coming chapters. Church leaders should see such resources as gifts.[1]

You may not have as much experience as you would like to handle this situation, but people with more experience are not

---

1. See Appendix C: National and State Domestic Abuse Resources for a good start on finding experienced and trained local resources in domestic abuse. Please take advantage of these resources. You cannot carry this burden alone.

sitting in the seat God placed you in at this time. You are in the position to help, and they are not. So learn from them, and help. By proximity, the burden to help is yours to bear (Gal. 6:2), but you should not bear it alone. You don't have to be an expert in domestic violence to respond competently.

I need to believe the best about people.
The process of caring for victims of domestic abuse often stalls before it even gets on the road. The point at which it often stalls is the initial disclosure, when a victim (or her friend) describes the cruelty of a man who is really a nice guy at church. To the church leader hearing the accusation, it may initially feel uncharitable to even consider the claim. It feels unloving to entertain the thought.

But this is an occasion where charitable instincts are wrong. A biblical view of people demands more from us. Christian love has more dimension to it than the flat pietism of 'believing the best about people.' Such pietism is often not much more than the vanilla tolerance of our age. Christians understand sin not just as external actions, but as inner corruption (Eph. 4:22). Christians also understand love not just as kind sentiments, but as the resolve to do what it takes to bring actual good to another person (1 John 3:18). So doing actual good for someone will sometimes involve not focusing on what they're doing right, but exposing what they're doing wrong (Heb 3:12-13). The self-deceit that is part of all sin is especially blinding in abusive sin. The more a person is self-deceived, the more taking him at his word is actually unloving. It allows him to maintain his illusion. God calls us to be discerning about people and their character, and to relate to them accordingly (Prov. 26:4-5, 24-25).

I'm not sure who is telling the truth in this situation.

You're right. You aren't sure. But you don't need to be certain about the truth to help. Unlike God, we discover truth through active exploration of the unfolding situation over time. If you waited to act until you knew who was telling the truth, you would be waiting a long time. And you would be acting too late for the sake of the victim.

False reports of abuse are rare, due to the stigma and shame associated with it. In fact, most experts say that abuse is typically under-reported. For this reason, we encourage first responders to take disclosures of abuse seriously. The truth will get sorted out through a coordinated community response in which there are multiple eyes on the relationship from many angles. We will not be recommending punitive measures toward a person accused of abuse without due process, but acting for the safety of a potential victim is not a question of punitive action of any kind. It is prudence.

More on that in the coming chapters. We will offer a framework to help you discern the best actions to take based on the limited knowledge you have at each stage. God does not expect you to be God. He alone knows the hearts of men. But, He does expect you to actively seek the knowledge necessary to make the hard decisions that, in faith, need to be made in a world of fallen relationships. Better yet, He will help you do it.

Why Active Involvement Is God's Will for Church Leaders

God gave leaders to the church to shepherd, protect, comfort, teach, guide, warn, and admonish them. They are examples to the flock of how Christians ought to conduct themselves in a world that doesn't look much like the God who made it. For our present concern, we want to highlight two particular ways church leaders model God's character.

Church leaders embody the protective care of the Lord to hurting people.

> I am the good shepherd. The good shepherd lays down his life for the sheep (John 10:11).

Christians have always found this to be one of Jesus' most beloved testimonies about Himself. We love it because it conveys how deeply He loves us—enough to face any danger that threatens His sheep. He is defensive of those who are His. They are weak. But He is strong. Church is where our families learn to sing this.

And church is where they see it modeled. Jesus calls Himself the Good Shepherd, but He extends His care through under-shepherds. He places them over His church to model His care—to love the sheep He loves with the same protective heart. You hear this in the apostle Paul's voice as he speaks his parting words to the elders he appointed in Ephesus, 'Pay careful attention to yourselves and to all the flock, in which the Holy Spirit has made you overseers, to care for the church of God, which he obtained with his own blood. I know that after my departure fierce wolves will come in among you, not sparing the flock' (Acts 20:28-29).

Paul describes these wolves as coming 'from among your own selves' who go around 'speaking twisted things' in order 'to draw away disciples after them' (v. 30). Paul was warning them of men who would both *teach false doctrine* and *live falsely before the people* (2 Cor. 11:1-15; Gal. 1:6-9; 1 Tim. 6:3-5; 2 Tim. 3:1-9). The two always go together. False teachers exert their influence through both *teaching* and *behavior*.

Church leaders are charged with protecting the flock from false teachers. Perhaps you only considered false teachers as those who would try to teach some ancient heresy in Sunday School class. Those are not the people 'from among your own selves' you typically need to worry about. Those problems are apparent, and you have a doctrinal statement to help you draw the proper lines. No, the more typical danger to your people are those who, with their influence, *live falsely* before them. They may never get behind a lectern or hand out pamphlets, but they still teach. In fact, they teach far more effectively by modeling with their private behavior lies about who God is, what marriage was designed for, even what love is. When false living involves violence, the destructive effects mushroom.

Protecting God's people is not easy. You are entering into a risky situation. We will offer suggestions for a wise approach that reduces certain risks, but the threat is real. Jesus is not a hired hand who flees when the wolves come (John 10:13). The shepherds He appoints don't flee either. This is why you must respond resolutely when abuse is disclosed or the possibility of abuse becomes evident. Vague responses will not disrupt the anything-but-vague dynamic of abuse that vulnerable people endure. Unflinching response comes from strong resolve and clear perception. Strong resolve comes from sharing the Good Shepherd's heart. Clear perception comes from understanding the dynamics involved. You are reading this book to begin forming that perception.

Church leaders use their influence to serve the church, never to take from her.
The apostle Peter, as bold a leader as he was, spoke of the responsibility of oversight tenderly, even poetically in 1 Peter 5:2-3:

Shepherd the flock of God that is among you, exercising
oversight,
not under compulsion,
but willingly as God would have you
not for shameful gain,
but eagerly
not domineering over those in your charge,
but being examples to the flock.

Peter's threefold contrast shows how easily that responsibility
can be misused. This is why many people have rejected the
very idea of authority—they cannot separate authority from
its misuse. They may never have seen a good example of godly
authority, in which the person in authority willingly takes on
the responsibility to provide for others instead of himself, and
the decisions he makes are for their gain and not his own.

Peter had learned from his Master. Power is never exercised
for the gain of the one who possesses it, but for the gain of those
who don't. Authority is exercised *at cost* to the one in authority.
I imagine Peter remembered with some ache in his soul the
rebuke of Jesus, when the disciples were elbowing past each
other for more authority.

You know that those who are considered rulers of the Gentiles
lord it over them, and their great ones exercise authority over
them. But it shall not be so among you. But whoever would
be great among you must be your servant, and whoever would
be first among you must be slave of all. For even the Son of
Man came not to be served but to serve, and to give his life as
a ransom for many (Mark 10:42-45).

Jesus, the Son of God, used His authority to give His life for
our gain, not to take our lives for His gain. But that's not all.
After He had given His life, He was raised from the dead and
granted all authority in heaven and earth as the risen Son of

Man sitting at the right hand of God (Matt 28:18; Eph 1:20-23). The manner in which He exercises His authority from this new position of privilege is the same: to bring life to those under it.

People who live under abuse experience the exact opposite. Whether an abusive person uses the word 'authority' or not, he uses greater influence (whether due to greater physical strength, earning potential, social connectedness, or otherwise) to gain from those with less. This is an evil authority. And evil authority is not combated with the absence of authority (which is a fantasy that ends up causing greater harm to vulnerable people). No, evil authority is combated with godly authority.

By displaying self-emptying authority, church leaders create an atmosphere that's oxygen to victims and survivors of abuse. The apostle Paul makes this connection. At church, godly authority is displayed when pastors—and by implication, all church leaders—are self-controlled, not violent but gentle, not quarrelsome, not greedy for personal gain, not arrogant, not quick-tempered, not a drunk, and able to display the kind of leadership that rallies his family behind him rather than exasperates them (1 Tim. 3:1-7; Titus 1:6-9; Eph 6:4). This is oxygen to people living under abuse, who have to go home to deadlier air.

And as much as godly influence is oxygen to victims of abuse, it is carbon monoxide to abusers. The Lord, the ultimate authority, has never tolerated for very long the oppression of His people by the powerful people of this world.

> For he who avenges blood is mindful of them;
>   he does not forget the cry of the afflicted.
> (Ps. 9:12)

Remembering those who are afflicted requires a form of avenging—not going on some crusade or leveling threats at an abuser, as we'll explain. No, the concept of avenging is when the damage done is accurately accounted for, leading to the appropriate action to right it. You will learn that an abuser is unable to account for the damage he has done, and a victim of abuse is unable to take action in righting it.

Godly authority takes on the responsibility of both. And the relieving news for you is that this authority does not belong to you. It is derived from Christ, the ultimate authority.

Conclusion

When the situation feels overwhelming, it's helpful to remember that you didn't put yourself here. You are only trying to respond in the wisest way possible, caring for everyone who is involved, especially the victim.

If the Lord has called you to care for people, He will be with you as you do it—however confused or clumsy you feel. The Lord is not confused or clumsy, and He will be with you. You are just His agent. An agent of His love. He will love you through this process, so that you can carry that love wisely into the lives of others.

So what does it mean to love wisely in a terrible situation like this? It starts with understanding the people caught up in it.

2

Understanding Abuse Dynamics

Of all the social problems confronted by the church, domestic violence is surely one of the most misunderstood and mismanaged by church leaders.—Steven Tracy[1]

Speak up for those who have no voice,
  for the justice of all who are dispossessed.
Speak up, judge righteously,
  and defend the cause of the oppressed and needy.
(Prov. 31:8-9, CSB)

You may be reading this book as a church leader or Christian friend who wants to know how to respond helpfully when someone discloses that abuse is occurring in her home. This

---

1.   Steven Tracy, 'Clergy Responses to Domestic Abuse,' *Priscilla Papers*, 21:2 (Spring 2007), 9.

chapter contains some essential information about abuse dynamics you will need to act wisely toward people caught up in those dynamics.

It's also possible you are reading this book because you have been, or are currently, in an abusive relationship. We hope this book is an encouragement to you, helping you understand abuse dynamics and what church leaders can do to help. The terms and descriptions in this book may or may not line up entirely with your experience. Our aim is to help others understand what you're going through so that they can take wise action on your behalf as agents of God's love. But always remember that God understands everything we can't.

So let's start with a brief word about terminology, since this is where it's all too easy to get stuck, then miss arriving at a deeper understanding of what's going on.

A Brief Word on Terminology

The words we use are important. So let's remember a basic truth about words: they are neither rock nor vapor. They're more like elastic. In other words, the meaning of a word is not set rock-like, so that it is the same in every context or in every person's intention in using it. But words are also not vapor-like, as if their meaning had no grounding in common use or can shift forms for no reason. They are elastic—a solid material that stretches to a certain degree, but no further.

Terms like *abuse, abuser, victim,* and *survivor* each have a variety of meanings in domestic abuse literature. These terms can be helpful, but only as circumstantial identifiers, not core identities. Helpful uses of these terms are simply circumstantial descriptions of a person in relation to the abuse that occurred. Unhelpful uses are identifiers that define a person entirely by their relation to the abuse that occurred.

For instance, a *victim* is a person on the receiving end of abuse and therefore suffering the direct effects of the harmful actions of another; yet, her entire identity is not captured by this term. Insofar as this term helps a person understand what occurred to her and the consequences on her life, it is helpful. Insofar as it becomes the inalterable center of her identity, it is unhelpful.

An *abuser* is the one on the giving end of abuse and therefore responsible for the harmful effects he inflicts on others; yet, his entire identity is not captured by this term either. Insofar as this term alerts a person to the extremity of his behavior and the corrupted heart behind it, it is helpful. Insofar as it becomes a sweeping dismissal of his personhood, it is unhelpful.

Throughout this book, we will use masculine pronouns for abusers and feminine pronouns for victims, since males are statistically much more likely to perpetrate abuse and females much more likely to be the victims.[2] This convention is used in most, if not all, the literature on domestic abuse that we have read and studied. However, we do understand that there are cases in which the abuser is female and the victim is male. It is not our desire to overlook the hurt experienced by males who have been oppressed. Husbands can live under the violence—sometimes subtle and sometimes explosive—of wives who attempt to control them through whatever means they can. The main dynamics of abuse are similar, but with a few unique aspects, which we briefly outline in Appendix F. If you are helping with a situation involving an abusive wife and

---

2. It is generally accepted in the domestic abuse literature that, overall, far more women than men are victims of domestic abuse. According to the Bureau of Justice Statistics, over 80 percent of criminal domestic abuse victims during the period 1993-2011 were female. See Shannan Catalano, *Intimate Partner Violence: Attributes of Victimization, 1993-2011* (Washington, DC: U.S. Department of Justice, Office of Justice Programs, Bureau of Justice Statistics, November 2013), 3.

an abused husband, we hope that this appendix will help you wisely apply the principles and practices we recommend in the rest of the book.

Don't shy away from the helpful uses of any of these terms, but be mindful of the human tendency to settle into a label. Labels have the effect of making us feel like we have a generalized understanding of a situation. Humility gives us eyes for the intricate shades and hues of human experience that help us show love to the individuals in front of us who uniquely bear the image of God.

A Brief Word on Biblical Application

From the terminology we use to the concepts behind those terms, Scripture is our ultimate authority. So how do we understand Scripture's authority over our terms and concepts? How does Scripture direct the way we understand human experience, including domestic abuse?

Even someone with a sincere desire to apply Scripture well may sometimes apply it poorly, especially to complex issues like domestic abuse. In fact, the more complex the issue, the clearer you have to be in your method of applying Scripture. So let us lay out what our methodology is and what it is not.

Let's start with what it is not. We are not merely attempting to find *domestic abuse* as a keyword or even a theme in Scripture, as if Scripture describes domestic abuse somewhere if we just hunt for it hard enough. Since the term domestic abuse is not in Scripture, we may be tempted to look for the closest analogous terms, then piece together Scripture's supposed description of domestic violence. Terms used in Scripture such as *violence, oppression, harm, unfaithfulness,* and *sin* can be used (and will be used by us) to illuminate aspects of domestic abuse, but none of these terms capture the entirety of the experience of domestic abuse. They weren't meant to.

Or, we may be tempted to look for stories that portray domestic violence as a way of determining how Scripture speaks to the experience. This attempt turns up little material, so we'd have to settle for situations that come closest. But they're all a stretch: such as the disturbing account of Lot offering his own daughters to be sexually abused by the ravenous men of Sodom (Gen. 19:8) and the similar story of another man handing his concubine over to be brutalized by the men of Gibeah (Judg. 19:16-21). Or, Amnon raping his half-sister Tamar, then shaming her (2 Sam. 13:1-22). These all have elements of violence in a domestic situation, but these stories do not capture the dynamics of ongoing domestic abuse. They weren't meant to.

Scripture works far more richly than this in addressing the situations of life. Rather than merely *describe* the situations we find ourselves in, Scripture *provides a perspective to view* our situations through.[3] Or better, we could say Scripture provides *a set of perspectives* to view our situation through. Or better still, Scripture provides a set of *authoritative* perspectives that should shape our own. The different themes of Scripture (doctrines, if you like) are these perspectives through which we view the problem of domestic abuse. Like looking at a problem from different angles, when these thematic perspectives are

---

3. We want to be clear: using keywords and narrative descriptions are an important part of biblical interpretation. We are simply pointing out that whenever we relate a present situation to either a keyword or a narrative in Scripture, we must pay attention to what is analogous and what is not. Terms like 'oppression' used in their redemptive-historical context are not equivalent to domestic abuse; though much of the conceptual content behind it corresponds, it does not equate. The same is true for the stories of Scripture. This is why we are suggesting that Scripture assembles a set of perspectives to see domestic abuse through.

assembled together, they offer a more dimensional picture of what is going on in domestic abuse. We'll go further out on a limb and say that these biblical themes offer the only *ultimately true* perspective of domestic violence, since they alone give us insight into God's ultimate perspective.

The problem we face in applying Scripture to domestic abuse is not that there isn't enough material to work with, but rather how to choose the best themes to prioritize in our perspective. The themes of Scripture are countless—creation, hope, transgression, judgment, kingdom, shalom, law, justice, deliverance, atonement, mercy, holiness, rest. Not only is this list a small sample, each one of them can be broken down into a number of smaller themes. The Bible is wonderfully immense.

Theology is forged by people trying to make sense of their world, and looking to the Word of God as their guide. In fact, theology has been called simply *the application of God's Word by persons to all of life.*[4] The following is our attempt to do this to the problem of domestic abuse. Many other themes of Scripture could offer complementary perspectives, but we've chosen what we consider to be the most essential for church leaders to respond wisely to domestic abuse.

What you will find below is our attempt to view domestic abuse through the pertinent biblical themes of:

1. The Image of God, displayed in our capacity both to perceive the world as persons and to influence one another as persons.

2. Sin, which disorders this design, warping both the ability to perceive the world rightly and to relate to others righteously.

---

4. John Frame, *The Doctrine of the Knowledge of God* (Phillipsburg, NJ: P&R Publishing, 1987), 76.

3. Love, which is God's design purpose for human relationships. It is the building up of another person at cost to self, which is the precise opposite of abuse.

4. Oppression, which is not generic suffering, but a unique form of suffering involving the intentional sin of those with greater capacity against those with less.

5. Marriage, which is God's arrangement for a man and a woman to live out an exclusive form of love in which a husband leads in sacrificing his interests for his wife, who follows him in freedom.

6. The Church, the Spirit-indwelled people of God who seek to be a community that honors what is true and good and thwarts what is false and evil.

Understanding Abuse Biblically

How might we describe abuse, given these biblical considerations? We don't do it by merely calling abuse *sin* and moving on. This would be like calling cancer a disease or methamphetamine a stimulant. Both labels are true, but inadequate to handle the complexity of these problems. The problem of abuse has its own particular dynamics.

Abuse is a sin that affects personhood, as God designed it. Here is our essential description of abuse, followed by an unfolding explanation of how these theological perspectives allow us to see the particular dynamics of abuse in their naked form:

Abuse occurs as a person in a position of greater influence uses his personal capacities to diminish the personal capacities of those under his influence in order to control them. Because God made people as embodied souls, these personal capacities are both physical and spiritual. Abuse is identified from two directions: (1) the manipulative intent and behavioral

39

forcefulness of the one in a position of influence, and (2) the diminishing effect on those under his influence.

Abuse desecrates the personhood of the one being abused. God created people in His image to represent Him in the world. This means every person is granted the privilege of using his or her personal capacities to bring order and goodness to the world as a representative of God (Gen. 1:26-31). All sin is a failure to be like God in the use of personal capacities, but abuse takes this a step further by seeking to diminish the personal capacities of someone else. Abuse desecrates what God made sacred: the personhood of those who bear His image (James 3:9).

More specifically, an abusive person uses his personal capacities to force other people to deliver on his personal desires. The force he exerts inflicts damage—that is, the effect of weakening someone to make them easier to control. We will describe the damage done by abuse as *trauma*. Trauma has long-lasting effects on victims of abuse. We will discuss trauma and its effects a little more later in this chapter, and we will also discuss it in Chapters 6 and 7. Sadly, the people most harmed by the abuser are those most dependent on him.

The greater the influence a person has over others, the greater the potential for harm. Jesus got most harsh with people of influence misusing their power to scandalize those under them. He spoke of millstones, ropes around necks, and deep water (Luke 17:1-2). The problem is not in the authority itself, but in the misuse of authority for self-serving, rather than self-giving, purposes. In other words, whatever authority exists in human relationships is a derived authority, given only for the purpose of serving the ones under authority rather than being served by them (Mark 10:42-45).[5]

---

5. Even the Almighty God, who rightly demands our obedience, never forces obedience through the diminishing of personhood, through manipulation and self-interest. No, God brings about obedience in

But abuse also blunts the personhood of the one doing the abuse. God gave people faculties that are like His, faculties by which we understand the world—specifically, the capability to think, to desire, and to make choices in response to the world around them. As a person thinks incorrectly, is motivated by deviant desires, and makes wrong choices, his perception becomes more and more corrupted, like a cataract on the lens of the eye. As these patterns of thought and action deepen, a person loses the ability to see the world as God sees it (Rom. 1:18-32; Eph. 4:18-19). This is how sin warps human perception in a general sense, but the corrupted perception of an abuser has a particularly dangerous quality. That corrupted lens is personal entitlement. He believes he is entitled to having his desires met, and treats other people accordingly.

This corrupted perception leads to dangerous ways of relating to others. Personhood is tied to that central purpose: to love God and to love others (Matt. 22:37-40). The more a person uses his strength in line with this purpose, the more he reflects the personhood of God. Consider the beauty of it. A small, God-like creature using his God-like capacities to build those capacities in others. But consider the horror of the opposite. A small God-like creature using his God-like capacities to diminish those capacities in others. And by doing so, he diminishes his own personhood. The more he uses his strength for the opposite of the purpose for which he was given it, the more he hardens into some alternate version of what he was meant to be.

His children through the restoration of their personhood by grace (2 Cor. 5:17-21). They are freed from their former constraints in sin to be all that they were created to be (Rom 6:1-23). God's authority is used for the benefit of those under it, and all human authority derives from God's and thus must conform to this same purpose, or it is illegitimate authority.

Abuse is a dangerous reversal of love. Trying to control others is not why God gives people personal strength. The Lord designed people with God-like faculties for one main purpose: to love. To be a bit more specific, love is using one's personal capacities to bring about good for others in the world—ordering it, caring for it, arranging it to bring about the greatest benefit not to oneself, but to other people. Love is the fulfillment of God's will for human relationships, and does no harm to a fellow image bearer (John 15:12-13; Rom. 13:8-10). Love helps others flourish at cost to self.

But abuse reverses this design. An abusive person uses his God-like faculties to overpower those same faculties in someone else to get what he wants. Instead of using his powers to arrange the world to God's glory, he uses his powers to arrange the world for his own. The more a person acts abusively, the more his perception is corrupted. The more his perception is corrupted, the more resistant to change his interactions become. Eventually, he loses the ability to perceive what love is and is not (1 John 4:20-21). His very personhood is diminished into a shell of what the Lord intended it to be.

Abuse is a form of oppression. The theme of suffering is ubiquitous in the Scriptures. God prepares His children to endure suffering in this world by trusting His care for them. God's Word teaches us that suffering produces sanctification (Rom. 5:3-4), that pain is purposeful (Rom. 8:28-29), that God comforts us in our suffering so that we can comfort others with the same comfort we have received (2 Cor. 1:3-4), that suffering is a gift (Phil. 1:29), and that we suffer because Christ suffered (1 Pet. 2:21), among other things. A theology of suffering is essential for a church leader, but a theology of suffering without considering God's view of, and response to, violence and oppression can lead to reckless care and harmful counsel.

God hates oppression, and we ought to pay close attention when Scripture tells us that God hates something. We should hate what He hates. 'The LORD tests the righteous, but his soul hates the wicked and the one who loves violence' (Ps. 11:5). In Scripture when the oppressed cry out to God, He hears them and He does something about it.[6] He displays His covenant loyalty to His people by opposing their harm at the hands of those who are stronger than them: 'The LORD is a stronghold for the oppressed, a stronghold in times of trouble...he does not forget the cry of the afflicted' (Ps. 9:9, 12b).

The primary deliverance from oppression that all believers have experienced is the deliverance that Christ came to bring

---

6. The stories and commands of Scripture display this. A number of stories show God's heart to the oppressed. When Sarai oppressed Hagar (Gen. 16), the angel of the LORD found her (v. 7), promised to multiply her offspring, providing protection and provision for her (v. 10), and told her that the LORD had listened to her affliction (v. 11). In response, Hagar calls Him 'a God who sees me' and says, 'Truly here I have seen him who looks after me' (v. 13). Or when Laban oppressed Jacob by deceiving him, changing terms, and otherwise manipulating him, Jacob responds to him, 'God saw my affliction and the labor of my hands and rebuked you last night' (Gen. 31:42). On a larger scale, when the Egyptians oppressed Israel with forced labor, decreased provisions, and increased demands, Scripture records, 'Their cry for rescue from slavery came up to God. And God heard their groaning, and God remembered his covenant with Abraham, with Isaac, and with Jacob. God saw the people of Israel—and God knew' (Exod. 2:23-25). A number of commands also show God's heart toward the oppressed: 'You shall not mistreat any widow or fatherless child. If you do mistreat them, and they cry out to me, I will surely hear their cry, and my wrath will burn, and I will kill you with the sword, and your wives shall become widows and your children fatherless' (Exod. 22:22-24). 'Thus says the LORD of hosts, Render true judgments, show kindness and mercy to one another, do not oppress the widow, the fatherless, the sojourner, or the poor, and let none of you devise evil against another in your heart' (Zech. 7:9-10). 'O LORD, you hear the desire of the afflicted; you will strengthen their heart; you will incline your ear to do justice to the fatherless and the oppressed, so that man who is of the earth may strike terror no more' (Ps. 10:17-18).

from the oppression of sin and its effects in the fall.[7] This is a comprehensive salvation, whereby God saves His people from the penalty of sin, but also trains them to oppose sin in their own lives and in the church, and beyond into the world. In other words, we begin to respond as God does when we see sin, including the sin of human oppression. God sees the oppressed, hears their cries, and acts with compassion, mercy, and justice. He tells us we should do the same: 'Thus says the LORD: Do justice and righteousness, and deliver from the hand of the oppressor him who has been robbed' (Jer. 22:3a). 'Open your mouth for the mute, for the rights of all who are destitute. Open your mouth, judge righteously, defend the rights of the poor and needy' (Prov. 31:8-9). And in the new covenant community, 'Bear one another's burdens, and so fulfill the law of Christ' (Gal. 6:2).

Abuse warps the purpose of marriage. This reversal of love is particularly dangerous in marriage because of what marriage was designed to be. God instituted marriage from creation as a union unlike any other type of human relationship (Gen. 1:24-25; Matt. 19:5-6). In this exclusive union, a man and a woman express love to one another by using their unique capacities to build the other up. God arranged marital love to be a particularly potent kind of love—where each spouse is formed into the fullness of what God made him or her to be.

Marital love is powerful. It is a union of complementary beings. To complement means to complete, which means a husband does not have in himself the particular abilities a wife does, and vice versa (Gen. 2:18-25). This union requires

---

7. Reading from Isaiah 61, Jesus inaugurated His ministry by pointing to Himself as the fulfillment of the text: 'The Spirit of the Lord is upon me, because he has anointed me to proclaim good news to the poor. He has sent me to proclaim liberty to the captives and recovering of sight to the blind, to set at liberty those who are oppressed, to proclaim the year of the Lord's favor' (Luke 4:18-19).

different kinds of contributions from a husband than from a wife. What we wish to emphasize for our present purpose is that Scripture describes the husband as particularly responsible for using his strength to build up his wife (Eph. 5:25-33). God intends a man to take the initiative in spending his efforts for the good of his wife. Her good is to be formed not into the image of her husband's preferences, but rather into what God determines for her individual calling to look like Jesus Christ.

But what is powerful for the accomplishment of good can be powerful for the accomplishment of evil. When a husband leads by using his capacities for the opposite purpose, for belittling his wife, he harms her in particularly destructive ways. And God holds him to stricter account.[8] What makes domestic abuse a particularly cruel form of violence is that the home is supposed to be the place where personhood blossoms into its greatest potential. When home hurts, the world suffers.

Abuse should be outrageous to the church. The home is not an island. In God's design of the church, families are not independent, self-contained kingdoms. They are accountable to a broader community. When a family insulates itself from community influence, those who are most vulnerable are put at greater risk.

---

8. Though far less common by reason of design, women can also use their strengths—physical, relational, intellectual—to weaken or diminish their husbands, causing lasting effects on him. Such situations require the same compassionate involvement we are encouraging for female victims. These situations also require awareness of the unique dynamics that may be in play—such as the stigma and shame associated with being a male victim and the potential incredulity of their community. We discuss this less-common dynamic in Appendix F. It is also quite possible that the dynamic that you may be observing is a more-common dynamic of abuse known as 'resistive abuse' or 'reactive abuse,' in which the female victim is simply trying to protect herself from further abuse. This is one of the reasons why it is important to have trained and experienced eyes and ears involved in your care of domestic abuse situations.

Here's how: The people who are most dependent on an abusive person suffer the worst consequences of his self-deception. As an abusive person relates to them out of this corrupted perception, he influences their perception of everything. Those under the influence of an abuser are bombarded with lies about God's intention for human relationships, causing all kinds of havoc in their perception of self, of others, and most tragically, of God. When this happens, the victims' capacity to see things rightly is diminished.

But God made the church to be the Spirit-indwelled people of the Word who are together learning to love what God loves and to hate what God hates. The beliefs and values conveyed in the pages of Scripture find their embodiment in living people. Jesus wanted the church to be the one type of community in all the world that demonstrates authority as self-emptying service for the good of those under it. In the church, greatness is demonstrated in servanthood (Matt. 20:25-28). When abuse is foreign and outrageous to God's people, the church is reinforcing God's perspective. This will help victims of abuse find their bearings.

Church leaders must actively guard their people from the deceit of abuse. Sadly, this is often not the case due to leaders being ignorant of the problem, being fearful of offending someone by sticking their noses in other people's business, or worst of all being abusive in their own way of thinking. But if you're a church leader reading this book, be encouraged that for your church, it can be different. By God's grace, it must be different.

Now that we've established an understanding of the dynamics of abuse, let's unpack some further insights into the people involved in abuse.

Understanding an Abusive Person

What might surprise you about abuse is that it has as much to do with *who a person is* as it does with *what a person does*. Abuse is a mindset as much as a behavior, a way of seeing as much as a way of behaving. To put it a bit more technically, abuse is corrupt perception as much as corrupt interaction. An abusive person is an image-bearer of God whose perspective of God, himself, and others is corrupted in particularly devastating ways, leading to warped ways of behaving.

Church leaders need to be aware of this diminished personhood if they are going to approach a potentially abusive person appropriately. This diminished capacity is seen in both his corrupted perception and his corrupted behavior toward those under his influence.

Corrupted Perception

Perception is simply the way a person sees the world. And the way he sees the world is determined by the contents of his heart— the beliefs and desires that act like lenses through which he sees everything. God made us to perceive the world accurately from true beliefs and desires. But ever since mankind's fall into sin, we have seen the world through corrupted beliefs and deceitful desires (Gen. 3:1-7; Rom. 1:18-32; Eph. 4:22). Sin warps everyone's ability to see the world rightly. But to varying degrees.

The degree is high for an abusive person. This makes sense, given God's design purpose for humanity being to love. The more contrary to love you act, the less you're able to understand the world as God sees it. This is called the hardening effect of sin—it diminishes a person's ability to see. Consider 1 John 2:10-11:

Whoever loves his brother abides in the light, and in him there is no cause for stumbling. But whoever hates his brother is in the darkness and walks in the darkness, and does not know where he is going, because the darkness has blinded his eyes.

The apostle John captures this dynamic perfectly: Acting hatefully toward others is a sure sign of spiritual blindness. They don't perceive what is obvious to others. In fact, John calls such people self-deceived (1 John 1:8). The nature of deception is that a person is unaware that they are being tricked. A self-deceived person is not aware he is seeing wrongly.

An abusive person usually sees himself as better than he is. He is not aware he sees himself wrongly, and his lens is always rose-tinted. He sees himself as *precise* instead of *nitpicking*. *Strong* instead of *brutal*. *Decisive* instead of *demanding*. *Tough* instead of *cruel*. He may be able to see when his actions go too far at times, but he acknowledges this more as a concession, an acknowledgement that 'nobody's perfect,' including himself. But admitting to wrong can still come from a dangerously shallow understanding of what he has become. He may even be full of self-loathing, but without open repentance, it is only his personal frustration with his own inability to be a better person. He's completely unaware of the extent of his self-deception.

An abusive person is also not aware he sees others wrongly. He sees them primarily in relation to what he wants from life, objectifying them and sizing them up according to whether they are a help or hindrance to him getting his own way. He is not usually doing this consciously, but intuitively. The more he acts toward them out of this perception, the more his interactions fall into a pattern. He loses the ability to recognize the original intention behind the behavior. He automatically interacts in a controlling way with those he perceives he can control, and differently toward those he perceives he cannot.

In the same way, an abusive person is not aware he sees God wrongly. There are many ways he might see God wrongly. He may think very little of God, and thus his abuse is carried out under the illusion that God is nonexistent or irrelevant. Or, he may think a lot about God—or rather, his version of God. God's standard of righteousness is basically the same shape as his own. God, then, is the justifying authority for this person's preferences. Instead of actively seeking to submit to Scripture, an abusive person will use Scripture to force submission from others. He believes he's seeing things biblically because he can connect certain Bible verses to what he wants to produce in someone else's life. He doesn't realize that using Scripture apart from its redemptive purpose is to misquote God.

Our point in this section is simply that you will only approach an abuser wisely if you are aware that he will be initially unable to see himself for who he is. Those who wish to minister wisely in these situations must take the hardening effect of sin seriously and not hide behind some simplistic view of sin as merely action that can be immediately identified, repented of, and moved past. This includes the hardening effect of sins done *by him* and *against him* in his past. We discuss this further in Chapter 8.

Corrupted Behavior Toward Others

If perception was merely a private matter, the corrupted perspective of an abuser would be dangerous only to himself. But people act out of their perception of the world. As we established earlier in this chapter, the Lord designed people with God-like faculties for one main purpose: to love. Love is using one's personal capacities to bring about good for others in the world.

A person should be considered abusive when he has established a pattern of doing the opposite: using personal capacities to force others to bring about good for himself. This can be called *control*. To control is to diminish the capacities of others so they're left in a position where they must conform. These attempts to control can be physical or nonphysical. An abusive person will manipulate others using whatever form of strength he has at his disposal—intellectual superiority, social superiority, spiritual superiority, financial superiority, conversational superiority, positional superiority, physical superiority, or any other form of advantage.

A thousand tactics of control can fall into any one of these categories, from subtle to explicit. Threats can be implied or outright and pertain to different types of harm—the threat of exposure, social ostracization, limited access to money, religious ridicule, bodily restraint or harm. When threats do not gain control over the individual, the abuser will initiate the threatened actions. He will often do this reluctantly, trying to preserve his own sense of moral cleanness. *I hate to do this, but you have forced my hand.* But eventually he gets over even that, and loses all sense of the wrongness of his action—unless he crosses a line of damaging his victim severely enough for others to notice. Then a flood of remorse disguised as concern for the victim will come out. This often fools the victim and the abuser alike into thinking that reconciliation has occurred.

An abuser's behavior should be understood as an attempt to gain control, that precious commodity that buys all his other desires. Like anyone else, an abuser will want many things out of life—power, affirmation, pleasure, peace, adventure, accomplishment—but what sets him apart from those who don't abuse is that he's figured out how to exert control as the means to gain those things.

Historically, domestic violence has been described in terms of a cycle of violence.[9] Though practitioners and interventionists are moving away from using this cycle to describe domestic abuse, we mention it here because of the tendency of Christians to mistake a part of this pattern for repentance. The stages have been described differently from study to study, but generally follow the movement from building tension, to an explosive event of some kind, to apparent remorseful (but not repentant) calm—then back through again, but incrementally worse each time. In such cases, an abusive person, and perhaps those who work with him, will perceive his remorse as an indicator that he's a good person who just has a problem. An abusive man familiar with Christian terminology, or a Christian leader, may even perceive this apparent remorse as real repentance. You must be aware that such a cycle, if it even exists in this particular case, is part of the hardening effect of sin, and adjust your approach accordingly. **Any appearance of change in a pattern of domestic abuse that is not sustained long-term and is not accompanied by evidence of new patterns is not repentance, and should not be judged as such.**

---

9. The seminal work on this topic was done by Lenore E. Walker, Ed.D., a licensed psychologist, and published in her groundbreaking 1979 book, *The Battered Woman* (New York: HarperCollins, 1979), 55-70. In Chapter 3, 'The Cycle Theory of Violence,' Dr. Walker identified three phases: the tension-building phase, the acute battering incident, and kindness and contrite loving behavior. This last phase is sometimes referred to as 'the honeymoon phase.' It is what the Bible calls worldly sorrow, but is sometimes mistaken by believers for godly sorrow. Mistaking worldly sorrow for godly sorrow can obviously be very dangerous. Scott Allen Johnson, another psychologist, built on Walker's work in his *Physical Abusers and Sexual Offenders: Forensic and Clinical Strategies* (Boca Raton: Baker & Francis Group, 2007), 31-51. In Chapter 6, 'The Offense Cycle Explored,' Johnson presents a more detailed fourteen-stage cycle, based on Walker's three phases. Lundy Bancroft has also explored Walker's three-phase cycle in his book, *Why Does He Do That? Inside the Minds of Angry and Controlling Men* (New York: Berkeley Books, 2002), 147-151.

You must also be aware that, while abuse is a patterned behavior, these patterns are highly nuanced and complex, often varying from case to case. For example, the problem with looking for a pattern that consists of an 'explosive event' is that you might be thrown off from seeing deeply destructive patterns of coercive control in which such an explosive event is not yet present. Whether or not physical or sexual abuse is ever present, the emotional pain is still quite real. Even if you do observe something of the patterns described above, be aware that the abuse has not stopped during a period of apparent 'remorseful calm.' Like Tolkien's character Beorn, the 'skin-changer,' it has just changed its form. But, unlike Beorn, who could only change from bear to man and back, abusers can often deftly shape-shift into a variety of forms. And victims and their advocates will tell you that such a remorseful period rarely, if ever, feels anything at all like a honeymoon. And as for the tension, most victims and their advocates will often tell you that it is almost always present and chronic, and its unpredictability and ever-changing form is confusing, disorienting, and unnerving.[10]

Abusers do not fit into a single personality profile, and their attempt to gain control will not always look the same. This is why describing patterns of abuse according to any one model can be dangerous. They can be outgoing or reserved, intelligent or dim, ambitious or lackadaisical. Some abusers are more aware of their calculations, and some are less—like criminal

---

10. For more information on the ongoing, constant nature of domestic abuse and coercive control, including what he calls 'arbitrary deprivations of liberty,' read Evan Stark, *Coercive Control: How Men Entrap Women in Personal Life* (New York: Oxford University Press, 2007). The insidious 'silent' and 'invisible in plain sight' forms of coercion, such as monitoring her time and movements, isolating her from friends, not allowing her to leave the home, and controlling decision-making, can be far more damaging than the more overt forms of abuse. Stark asserts that coercive control is actually a better predictor of domestic homicide than overt violence.

masterminds versus thugs. Many abusive individuals are quite adept at impression management. It is likely that he might be the type of person in your church or small group that everyone would describe as charming, kind, or generous in public. The point is, you do not identify an abuser by the form he shifts into at church or at work or any other place in which he wants to create a positive impression, but by behaviors committed behind closed doors that 'frighten, intimidate, terrorize, exploit, manipulate, hurt, humiliate, blame, injure, or wound an intimate partner.'[11] In other words, an abuser is known by his use of his personal capacities to limit the personal capacities of those under his influence to get what he wants.

You're looking for patterns of a person exerting this kind of control. But keep in mind how this type of knowledge will come to you. You don't gain immediate knowledge of the pattern as a whole, but usually as piecemeal disclosures of concerning behavior, some of which will seem less severe than others. But realize that controlling behaviors do not happen in isolation. The pattern will never be smaller than the specific incidents, and is almost certainly larger. A person being victimized by abuse often does not have the whole pattern mapped out in her own mind, let alone the ability to communicate it in a comprehensive and succinct way to a people-helper trying to care for her. For more on this, let's consider how to understand a person being abused.

Understanding the Person Being Abused

A victim is an image-bearer of God who carries in her body and soul the devastating scars of another person's controlling

---

11. Justin S. Holcomb and Lindsey A. Holcomb, *Is It My Fault? Hope and Healing for Those Suffering Domestic Violence* (Chicago: Moody, 2014), 57.

and abusive behavior toward her. These wounds of both soul and body, which can also be called 'trauma,' impact both her perception and her behavior. This is in keeping with our theologically-informed perspective of abuse: we exist to bring glory to God by loving Him and others. Abuse dishonors God by desecrating His image in the other person. The impact of the desecration of the image of God in the victim is what we are describing in this section.

When we say that she carries this trauma in her body, we are not simply referring to wounds from overt physical or sexual aggression that are physical in nature, although those may certainly exist. We are also referring to the countless potential physiological manifestations of trauma and stress: panic attacks, fatigue from constant hypervigilance or from disturbed or restless sleep, chronic pain, changes in appetite, unexplained aches and pains, and digestive issues, among other manifestations. You can encourage victims to learn to be more aware of, and to take care of, their physical bodies, as the Lord does. But also be aware that, in some cases, the abuser may be limiting her medical care. And, in other cases, she may be resistant to certain elective medical care either because of the abuse or out of fear of the abuse being discovered. Be sensitive to these potential factors.

When we say that she carries this trauma in her soul, we are referring to the soul-crushing emotional and spiritual effects of her abuse, such as feelings of deep worthlessness and shame, difficulty regulating emotions, re-experiencing the traumatic events in response to triggers, hypervigilance, shutting down emotionally, troubles with concentration and memory, and the corrupted perceptions of self, God, and others that we will discuss later in this chapter.

The victim's perception and behavior, corrupted by the abuse she has endured, may sometimes not make much sense to someone who hasn't endured similar abuse, or who is unfamiliar with trauma. It may even lead you to believe that she is the one with the problem, a belief that her abuser is sure to reinforce. She doesn't want your pity, just your understanding, compassion, encouragement, and empathy. She has proven herself strong and resilient to have survived the abuse for this long. Everyone's experience of abuse is different, so this section is just meant to provide an overview. The best way to understand the impact of trauma on a particular person is to gently and sensitively ask her about it when she is ready to talk. We will discuss how to care for her more in later chapters. For now, we just want to give you some general idea of how the abuse may have affected her.

Perception Corrupted by Abuse

As we described earlier, those under the influence of an abuser are bombarded with lies about God's intention for human relationships, causing all kinds of havoc in their perception of self, of others, and most tragically, of God.

The stories that victims tell themselves about their abuse are accompanied by a swirl of deeply entrenched cognitive, emotional, spiritual, and physical responses. Some abused spouses gravitate toward excuse making, some toward shame, and some toward despair. Others may take comfort in an overly spiritualized view of themselves as noble enough to endure anything in the name of love or even for the sake of the gospel. Others will be anxious, even terrified. And others will have reached the point where they have hardened into a deep cynicism toward the world. On any given day, a person can experience any combination of these.

Here are some common false stories that abuse can write in a person:

I am not a victim since this is not really abusive.
Either from a lack of knowledge or due to the sheer weight
of having to acknowledge that things have gotten this bad,
victims of abuse can minimize the dynamics that exist in
the marriage. You must be gentle with a victim who finds it
difficult to acknowledge the weight of what's happening to her.
Your job is to have clear eyes about what she is telling you about
how her home hurts, and to give her time and space to process
it for herself. You may utilize the principles from this book to
offer her another perspective on her experience by asking good
questions, listening well, and reflecting what you are hearing.

I am not a victim since I deserve this.
Sometimes a person will not see herself as a victim because
of shame. She may acknowledge that her spouse goes too far
sometimes, but she can always pinpoint what she did wrong
to trigger the violence. Her own shame keeps her from
acknowledging her present reality. Shame tells the story that
my fundamental identity is defined by my experience, by what
I have done, or by what has happened to me. It is an identity
statement. One that is not true, but deeply held, often because
it has been reinforced by the abuse itself. The problem here is
that she has adopted the standards of the abuser, standards that
collide with God's standards. In other words, she is accepting
a moral code radiating not from the righteous God, but an
unrighteous man. You can gently help her see her identity
from God's perspective as an image-bearer and, if redeemed
by Christ, as a daughter of the King. She is worthy of dignity,
honor, and value. She does not deserve the abuse she is enduring.
No image-bearer of God does.

I am not a victim. I am a sinner.
Sometimes people who understand that the Bible's central
message of the gospel is that Christ came to save sinners will

misapply that message to their situation. The story she tells herself is: *Since my main problem is sin, my main identity is as a sinner who needs redemption. Seeing myself as a victim contradicts this.* But this is an oversimplification. She can be both a sinner and a sufferer; we all are. One can be simultaneously a sinner in need of redemption and a victim of the cruelty of another person. The category of victim is not a secular idea that opposes the biblical idea of personal sin. Rather, it acknowledges a more robust understanding of sin's dynamic as having relational, social, and generational consequences beyond the individual.

I am a victim and will always be.
She may be living in a story in which her status as a victim feels permanent to her. Sometimes this has a flavor of shame, sometimes it has a flavor of despair, sometimes it has a flavor of numb resignation. Regardless, this is a false and unhealthy narrative that may lead to passivity, as we describe below. A person living in this story must be gently guided to acknowledge her victimhood as God sees it: a tragic form of suffering that doesn't have to continue. This does not mean the burden of changing her situation rests entirely on her—her options may in fact be quite limited—but it does mean that mere passive acceptance is harmful to both her and her abuser.

I am nothing but a victim.
Some people endure abuse so long that they actually adopt a victim mentality. By that, we mean that they see their status as a victim as a core feature of who they are. This may give her comfort as a sort of righteous sufferer. It may give her an unrecognized excuse not to face the difficult, and sometimes dangerous, task of removing herself from the abuse. Later on, if and when she removes herself from the immediate threat, a victim mentality may continue to affect her other relationships. She may see herself through this lens as she relates to others—

which can result in the polar tendencies to gravitate toward people who will harm her again or to perceive harm from people who are only trying to help her. This is perhaps one of the cruelest ways abuse can affect a person's perception: Since the residual effects on relationships are often too subtle to address, they can continue for the rest of a person's life, actually distancing her from others. The love she was created to give and to receive is hampered by a diminished view of self as primarily a victim, when she is so much more than this in God's eyes. In God's eyes, she is more than a victim—even more than a *survivor*, a term used often in domestic violence literature to describe a victim who is healing from her abuse. This is not a bad term, but we would suggest that *overcomer* may capture a bit more of what faith in Christ can mean for someone who has been victimized. We will say more in the coming chapter on how practically to help someone harmed by abuse.

A victim of abuse has been lied to about who God is and what He intends for human relationships. What has been modeled for her in painful detail is not love, but its tragic opposite. In spite of all she has been through, you may find in her a strong, resilient faith. If she is a believer, God has likely been a rock and a refuge to her in a time when little else has felt certain. If her abuse has cast her into a dark night of the soul or caused her to question God's character, this is a common human response to suffering. God is not afraid of her questions, fears, or doubts. We know that God has been ministering to her in profound ways long before you even become aware of her situation because He is 'near to the brokenhearted and saves the crushed in spirit' (Ps. 34:18). Your first job with her is to mirror the Lord's nearness. Don't make assumptions about her, but explore the false stories she has been living out enough to point her to the better and truer story. We will provide practical instruction on this in the next chapter.

Behavior Corrupted by Abuse

The false stories that shape an abused person's perception are then expressed in action. Victims of abuse are, of course, responsible for their responses—recognizing this is essential to honoring them as persons made in the image of God. Yet, we must acknowledge, as Jesus did, that the actions done to her by someone with greater influence has a traumatizing effect that a person can't escape. You can't close a person's fingers repeatedly in a closet door as punishment for leaving it open without establishing strong emotional associations with everything from that door to any other household duty she's instructed in. That's the whole intention of the abuser. Here are some common unhelpful behaviors that abuse can condition a person to do:

A victim of abuse may withdraw.
Whether because of shame or because her past attempts to let others in on the secret have failed, many victims of abuse withdraw from regular relationships. She may feel so foolish or ashamed of being in an abusive relationship that she would rather put up with the abuse than go through the embarrassment of having everything out in the open. When asked about her home, she may seem incoherent or evasive. In many cases, she may have tried to disclose the abuse but was not taken seriously. Pastors or church friends may have implied that she was exaggerating. They may have advised her to adjust her own behavior to make abuse less likely. Or they simply may have failed to follow up at all. Rather than push for attention she doesn't want in the first place, she may simply withdraw. Social isolation is also a tactic used by abusers to maintain greater control. If this is a component of the abuse she has experienced, she may have grown so accustomed to the lack of social interaction that she no longer even desires it.

A victim of abuse may struggle to regulate her emotions.
Another reason that victims sometimes isolate and withdraw is
that they find their emotions unmanageable. The anger, fear,
loss, betrayal, guilt and sadness may feel overwhelming to her
at times. Since she is overwhelmed with them, she assumes that
this flood of emotions will be overwhelming to you too. You
can care for her by being a calming, caring presence. Let her
know that you are not overwhelmed by her emotions. Let her
know that it makes sense that she would be angry, or afraid, or
sad. Weep with those who weep (Rom. 12:15). Be angry with
her about the abuse that has occurred (as God is), and model
for her how to be angry without sinning (Ps. 4:4; Eph. 4:26).
Give her a safe place to grieve, to cry, and to talk about her
fears.

*A victim of abuse often spends a great deal of her time and mental
energy trying to adjust to the abuser's often unpredictable patterns
of behavior. This is exhausting.*
As we described above, though abusive behavior does tend to
follow a pattern, these patterns are not as predictable as you
might think—often by design. Abusers sometimes like to keep
their victims guessing. Whether the abused spouse can describe
this explicitly or not, she has likely learned intuitively to read
his mood and the threat level and adjust accordingly. And
the more unpredictable his pattern is, the more anxious she
becomes. When some type of abusive incident does occur, she
may try to simply endure it in hopes of getting through; trying
to de-escalate him through apologies, self-blame, and promises
to do better; or by some sort of escape from the scene. When
an incident is over, she may adjust her behavior in a number
of common ways, from immediate reconciliation to trying to
exert the temporary sway she has over him while he still feels

his fleeting guilt. All of this makes for a volatile way of living, in which she is constantly adjusting herself to his reactions.

A victim of abuse may be hypervigilant.
Because of the abuser's unpredictable behavior, the victim may be constantly on high alert about what may set him off. It may seem that her head is constantly 'on a swivel,' looking for dangers and threats that may not even seem plausible to you. The threat level is quite real to her, and it is one of the clear markers that a traumatic event has occurred. The effects on body and soul of living continually in a heightened state of anxiety are profound over time. Being a calm presence and holding space for her may help to quiet the alarm bells that constantly ring in her head.

A victim of abuse may try to out-love, out-loyal, and out-last the abuse.
Sometimes the greatest defender of an abuser is the person being abused. You should not assume that an abused spouse will feel strong animosity toward her abuser. This may be part genuine love, part genuine fear, and part genuine naiveté. An abused wife will often feel a strong bond toward and affection for her husband, even having pity for him. This is sometimes called 'trauma bonding.' She may also be scared of allowing a disloyal thought to enter her mind, lest he somehow read it on her face. This is quite likely just a self-protective intuitive response. She may also think that love will somehow conquer the demon inside him, if she can just show him that he can count on her no matter what. Part of your job will be helping her to gain a biblical perspective of love, of fear, and of the difficult reality of sin's hardening effect on the soul of her abuser. Her love cannot change him. God must change him, and He will only do so through the means He describes in His Word: the pain of accountability. True love does not wish to spare him from

consequences, but rather allow consequences to do their good work. 'Do not be deceived: God is not mocked, for whatever one sows, that will he also reap' (Gal. 6:7).

A victim of abuse may seem to turn against those who try to help her.
It is possible that a victim of abuse may even go so far as to turn against those who are trying to help her. Don't take this personally, as if it is about you. She may be afraid, she may be ashamed, or she may just not trust you yet. You might ask about her concerns. You might give it time. Or, you might just not be the right caregiver for her at this time.

Under no circumstances should you attribute any of these effects of abuse to the victim herself or her personal sin. As you can see, the abuser, and often the victim herself and some of her helpers, are already doing that. We do not want you to be like Job's 'worthless healers' (Job 13:1-5). If it is an effect of the abuse, then it is suffering, not sin. We wrote this section because we wanted you to have some idea of what her world may be like. But, ultimately, the best way to know about her world is to ask her about it, and then listen well and ask good follow-up questions, which we encourage you to do. You might want to start with a simple, open-ended question like, 'What is it like to be you?'

Moving Forward

This was a difficult chapter full of difficult and complex realities. But we must seek to understand them if we are to move forward with wise action. Discerning where to start will be the topic of the next chapter.

3

Discerning Abuse Dynamics

When I was a child, I asked my parents why our house needed walls…. Their answer was simple: to keep the bad stuff out and the good stuff in…. In an abusive relationship, things flip. There walls are built to keep the bad stuff in and the good stuff out. —Helen Thorne[1]

Rescue those who are being taken away to death;
    hold back those who are stumbling to the slaughter.
If you say, 'Behold, we did not know this,'
    does not he who weighs the heart perceive it?
Does not he who keeps watch over your soul know it,
    and will he not repay man according to his work?
(Prov. 24:11-12)

---

1. Helen Thorne, *Walking with Domestic Abuse Sufferers* (London, UK: Inter-Varsity Press, 2018), 7.

The driving purpose of this book is to equip you to take knowledgeable action to help people under threat of abuse. We have not yet got to the point of action. That begins in the next chapter. This chapter closes out the section on how to think about abuse before we walk you through how to start helping.

The first chapter was about how to understand your role, the second chapter was about abuse dynamics themselves, and now this chapter will provide a framework that will help discern those dynamics in actual situations.

Just to be clear, the action does not start just yet. Action will actually begin with the victim, not the abuser. The next chapter will describe how to care well for someone when she tells you that her home hurts. This chapter is giving you the remainder of the essential knowledge you need for even wrapping your head around what's happening in potentially abusive situations.

Priority of Value

The hardest decisions in life are the ones where legitimate values compete for priority. Discerning where to start upon hearing of the possibility of a domestic abuse situation is such a decision. When you hear someone alert you to the possibility of abuse occurring, your mind may immediately start to weigh the different values you want to maintain in your approach, such as the sanctity of the marriage relationship, the need to avoid false accusations, peace in the church community, and more.

We urge you to always prioritize the safety of any potential victim as your driving value. The other values will fall into place eventually in the process. To initially prioritize the privacy of the marital relationship or the communal peace that could be disrupted has the greater potential to do harm. Whereas making every effort to keep a potential victim safe, when done wisely, does not pose the same risk of harm. Whether you recognize it or not, any response you give will have an intrinsic prioritization to it. We are simply urging you to be aware of that fact, and to choose safety first.

This applies even if you are uncertain about whether a potential victim is thinking clearly or not. Regardless of your personal impression about how reliable her claim is, the priority driving how you respond to her should be on her safety. The framework we will provide in this section is intended to help you do just that in a way that is responsible with the other values in tension.

In the previous chapter, we established an understanding of the dynamics involved in abuse. Based on that understanding, this chapter will provide a framework for discerning the dynamics of the situation in front of you.

You are likely reading this book because you are trying to help someone who is in a situation you don't fully understand yet. This framework is intended to help you determine how to act for the good of a potential victim while weighing the implications for a potential abuser. A framework for assessing an abusive threat is important because the level of severity will coincide with the level of immediate response.

A Framework for Discerning Abuse Dynamics

In the last chapter we laid out a theological perspective of abuse. Now comes the tough part—unpacking this experientially. That means answering the question, *When is a person actually being abusive?*

All sin is to some degree relationally harmful, but not all sin is abusive. A person who tells you they are being mistreated by their spouse may or may not be describing abuse. How can you tell the difference? When is relational sin abusive, and when is it not? This section is our attempt to take the theological description of abuse laid out in the last chapter and use it to discern the situation in front of you.

What You're Not Doing by Trying to Discern

We need to make clear what you're *not* doing in trying to assess abuse dynamics before we describe what you are doing.

First, you're not trying to arrive at a definitive pronouncement of abuse before taking action, since the action you're taking is not punitive against anyone. Often times, church leaders get so caught up with the question, 'Should we really call his behavior against his wife *abuse?*' that they fail to deliberate about the more urgent matter of ensuring the safety of a potential victim. She shouldn't have to prove anything to be taken seriously and offered protection and guidance in the form of a safety plan. We explain in the next chapter how to do this.

For now, we are trying to make it clear that church leaders should not wait on answers to all their questions before helping a potential victim to arrange for her safety. Yes, you will eventually need to understand to what degree a spouse is acting abusively, and this chapter is intended to provide a framework to help you do just that. But seeking answers to those questions can only be responsibly done once a safety plan is in place. If your child tells you he saw a black widow spider in his bedroom, you take measures to ensure he's safe before you confirm whether he's right or not. It could be just a harmless black spider. But there's a reason you instinctively remove your child from the room before poking around to find out: the process of examining will itself increase the risk of danger, and you don't want your child to be exposed to that increased risk. If it ends up that he was mistaken, you still made the right move to ensure his safety based on the knowledge you had at the time.[2]

Second, your role is not to investigate. When we discuss how to address the situation, we will walk you through how to involve well-trained and experienced personnel to protect victims. But in keeping with the purpose of this chapter providing knowledge before action, we simply want to make this distinction for you: You are not a forensic investigator trying to make conclusive determinations about exactly what happened or who is or is not telling the truth. Your role is caregiving and accountability. You do not need to be a police officer or a lawyer to seek the information you need for responsible pastoral action, and you should cooperate fully with officers who are investigating criminal matters.[3] Well-trained victim advocates

---

2. To be clear, church leaders do not *remove* an adult victim from danger apart from with their consent. Church leaders should not overzealously insist that the woman leave when she believes it is safer to stay than to leave. The example above is intended to simply clarify that the point of protective action is not after all information is gathered, but before.

3. The framework we provide in this chapter is intended to help you take responsible pastoral action. As we will make clear in the next chapter, part of responsible pastoral action is encouraging someone who may be being victimized to use the resources available to her under the law for her protection and the protection of anyone else under threat. This includes mandatory reporting to law enforcement, and/or the appropriate state agency in cases involving helpless dependents like children, disabled, or elderly people living in the home.

    What this means specifically is that you should (1) make a potential victim aware of the resources available to her (see Appendix C) and (2) help her to make a plan to use them in a way appropriate to her situation. In most places in the United States, the adult victim of domestic violence is the one who determines whether police get contacted or not. This is largely because of the threat of retaliation against a victim if she remains under the influence of the abuser after police have become involved. You do not want to increase the threat to the individual, but decrease it. Unless you witness a crime occurring yourself or believe that the person is under imminent threat, you need to help her make a responsible decision for herself.

can be a tremendous asset in helping her (and you) navigate the subtleties of the specific situation.[4]

Third, your job is not merely to determine if sin has occurred. Often pastors and church leaders treat abusive situations like they would any other relational sin, believing that the gospel compels quick movement toward repentance and reconciliation. Abuse is indeed sin, but it's a particularly dangerous and entrenched sin that must be handled with additional cautions. Repentance is always appropriate, and reconciliation sometimes is, but both occur in very different ways in an abusive situation.

Scripture conveys a thick doctrine of sin, not a thin one. Reading these situations through a thin doctrine of sin is tempting, since no one wants to seem uncharitable to anyone or be accused of being judgmental. But doing so is loving neither to victims of abuse nor to abusers, since it does not bring about the hard truth that could lead to lasting repentance and change.

What You Are Doing by Trying to Discern

What you *are* trying to do is consider to what degree a person may be acting abusively against someone else. What makes this so difficult is that all sin done in relationship can in some way be considered harmful, from lying to yelling. Spouses mistreat one another frequently. But we instinctively know that not all lies are abusive, and not all yells are abusive. In other words,

---

Since we are not legal professionals, and since we are unfamiliar with the specific laws and statutes in your locality, we encourage you to avail yourself of local resources, and familiarize yourself with the laws of your state or country.

4. See Appendix C: National and State Domestic Violence Resources for more information on locating advocates in your area.

abuse is a sinful way to treat people, but not all sinful ways of treating people are abusive. How do we discern the difference?

The distinguishing mark between abusive sin and non-abusive sin lies in the *use of personal capacity to diminish the capacities of another person so that she can be more easily controlled.* To put it more simply, abuse occurs insofar as one person uses his strength to limit the strength of another. Abuse, therefore, has a greater degree of potential in relationships in which one person has more capacity, privilege, or authority than another.

An illustration may prove helpful for making this distinction. Basically, every nature documentary addresses the different types of interactions that exist between species. Whether it's sharks and seals or wolves and elk, it's the harmful interactions that get the most air time. But what you may not notice is that not all harmful interactions are of the same type.

In ecological relationships there are different types of harm. Some interactions are classified as *competition*, where harm is done to both species because they are working against one another for the same resources. Squirrels will compete with songbirds for the seed in your backyard feeder. By seeking what they want for their own benefit, the species harm the other, but not directly. You won't see a squirrel attacking a bird directly. The hostility between them centers on the resource, with the other species being a hindrance.

But other types of harm assume a more nefarious character. *Predation* and *parasitism* are types of harm that directly limit the capacities of one species for the other's gain. A predator will directly benefit from the destruction of its prey. Unlike the songbirds in your backyard, a red-tailed hawk harms a squirrel not by competing for seed, but by directly attacking it with superior strength. The harm caused by the predator is direct and explicit, using force to incapacitate the prey in order to take life from it. Similarly, a parasite will directly benefit from the destruction of its prey, but gradually. Unlike red-tailed hawks ending a squirrel's life all at once, botfly larvae attach themselves to squirrels as they dig in the soil, burrowing under their skin to feed on their blood. The harm done by a parasite is just as direct, but more subtle in its diminishing effect.

The difference between being a *competitor* and a *predator/parasite* illustrates the difference between non-abusive and abusive sin in relationship. All relational sin is a form of *competition*—preferring self to another. Ignoring, dismissing, edging out someone else to get at the limited resources we all want—time, money, attention, right-of-way. All of this is ugly and wrong. God hates self-seeking, rivalry, slander, insults, and envy (Matt. 5:21-24; Gal. 5:26; 1 Pet. 2:1). Such sinful behaviors are a misuse of God's design for relationships and cause real relational damage (James 3:14-16). We should think of all relational sins as *misuse*, though not all of them as *abuse*. Sins of misuse are harmful in a competitive sense. They are characterized by *me before you*.

Abuse is something more. The difference lies in the use of personal capacity to diminish another's capacity for personal gain. Being a predator and being a parasite are just different points on a spectrum of hostility—one explicit and acute, the other subtle and gradual. Some forms of abuse are so explicitly predatory that identifying them is tragically easy. But far more difficult to discern is abuse that's more parasitic in nature, when an abuser uses more subtle tactics to diminish the personhood of another over time. These sins are not just competition and selfishness. These sins are the wearing away of another person's ability to act in the world. Abuse is interaction characterized by something beyond *me before you*. It's characterized by *me over you*.

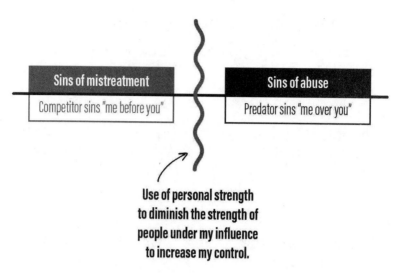

Use of personal strength to diminish the strength of people under my influence to increase my control.

In a real life situation, you won't find a hard line between sins of misuse and sins of abuse.[5] Graphs can't capture real life entirely. But we hope the principle laid out here is helpful for discerning abuse. If a person is using his personal abilities, privilege, strength, or influence to diminish those same things in someone else to make her easier to control, you are looking at an abuser.

This dynamic is particularly urgent to be mindful of in relationships where one person has greater capacity, privilege, or authority than another. As we tried to make clear earlier, it is not the differing levels of authority that creates abuse, but rather a greater potential for abuse. This is why God holds those with greater influence *more* responsible for the effect of their actions on others than the reverse.

---

5. This line of distinction is not merely the line between criminal and noncriminal acts. Yes, some types of physical abuse are criminal and must be handled with the involvement of legal authorities. But abuse can occur in ways that no police officer could arrest someone for. As a pastor or church leader, you must be aware of this, and not simply rely on the distinction between what the police would be involved with or not. The vast majority of domestic abuse is not illegal.

A Strategy for Discerning Abuse

Now that you have a general idea of the scale of abuse, let's zoom in a bit on the details. The following diagram simply adds details to the one above to be as useful as possible for discerning a real-life situation.

Remember, *you are determining if a person in some position of authority is using his power to diminish the power of another to get what he wants.* This means you will need to make a judgment call at two levels: the activity of the person with influence and the effects on the person under influence.

Influential Person Using Personal Capacities

FORCEFULNESS
PERSISTENCE
Less · More

To Diminish the Personal Capacities of Another

IMPACT ON BODY
IMPACT ON SOUL
Less · More

Unpacked further, you are considering:

1. **The Activity of the Person With Influence.** You are considering both (1) manipulative intent and (2) behavioral oppression, expressed in spiritual and physical ways.

- By *manipulative intent*, we mean the intention to gain personal control over the other. Notice that you are not trying to determine if a person *intends his actions to be abusive*, but rather that he *intends his actions to gain control over a person under his influence.* Abusive people may insist they don't intend abuse, assuming that this means they are not being abusive. This is a vital distinction to make when assessing the level of threat. But even more vital to pay attention to is the forcefulness of his behaviors toward a person under his influence.

- By *behavioral oppression,* we mean the degree of coercion the person's behavior has on those under his influence— namely, how much effort is being used to incapacitate another person's freedom of choice? It's vital to recognize that behavioral oppression occurs on a spectrum of greater and lesser degrees of both *forcefulness* and *persistence.*

- *Forcefulness* is the degree of threat a person faces for not conforming to the manipulative intent of the abuser. *Persistence* is the degree to which manipulative behaviors have established themselves as patterns in the relationship. The greater the degree of forcefulness and the greater the degree of persistence, the more clearly abusive a person's actions will be (physical assault regularly occurring for years).

- Behavioral oppression is both soul-impacting and body-impacting, since God made human beings embodied souls. One embodied soul is using his spiritual and physical capacities to hinder those same capacities in another.

- Regarding the soul, the behavior of an abusive person will include nonphysical interaction—primarily verbal and nonverbal means of communication. The words he says, the attitudes he displays with nonverbal cues, the money or time he spends on one activity over another—all of these can be utilized to manipulate those under him. A person can intimidate, guilt, badger, and corner someone without ever getting out of his armchair. The more forcefully the communication is used to gain control over another person for some desired end, the more abusive it is. Many have called this *verbal abuse, emotional abuse,* or *spiritual abuse.*

Those labels can be helpful and unhelpful. They can be helpful in acknowledging that abuse is not just physical. A person can seek dominance over another with words and relational maneuvers. But these words can be unhelpful in making false distinctions. Verbal abuse, for instance, is emotionally impactful, and emotions are an expression of spiritual activity. Instead, we are focusing our description of abuse on personhood as the image of God. Abuse is any diminishing of an individual's God-given capacities of personhood, including their ability to perceive rightly. Thus, abuse dynamics can occur without ever laying a finger on another person.

- Regarding the body, when an abusive person cannot adequately control others with words and maneuvers, he will often physically force his will on others. Threatening gestures (shaking a fist, slamming the wall next to someone) lead to acts that physically limit someone else (blocking an exit, gripping an arm, shoving). These acts can lead to more hostile behaviors that actively inflict pain (squeezing hard, smacking) and even do injury (punching, kicking). Left unchecked, this often results in extremely dangerous physical onslaughts (beating with fists, assaulting with other objects). All of these behaviors have a profound effect on the body—both visible (bruises, cuts, injuries) and invisible (traumatic reactions, physical problems from anxiety). This, too, is a diminishing of an individual's God-given capacities of personhood, since he made us to reflect His personhood as physical beings.

2. **The Effects on the Person Under Influence.** You are considering the diminishing effect on the person's ability to function in freedom of personhood, in both soul and body.

- You consider the effects on their soul—namely, how has their perception been diminished? More specifically, do their words, emotions, and behaviors show diminished freedom? In the previous chapter, we laid out how to understand the mentality of someone victimized by abuse. You are considering to what degree a person may be exhibiting that mentality.

- Perhaps most crucial to recognize is an established fear—a fear about what the other person can do to her, about any children that are in the home, about what her own failures seem to indicate about herself, or being rejected from her community if no one believes her. Remember, if abuse is going on, a victim will have been dominated with a number of relational maneuvers that will affect her ability to see her marriage, herself, and even God clearly.

- You also consider the effects on their body—namely, how has their health been diminished? The most obvious signs are physical injuries like bruises or abrasions. But less obvious diminishing effects on the body include chronic anxiety or depression and all the accompanying symptoms that go along with it. It can include fatigue, frequent illness, inability to concentrate, lack of motivation, and more. You don't need to be able to run a medical physical on a person; you just need to be aware that a victim's body can be impacted in ways that are not obvious.

All of these considerations occur on a spectrum of concern, with no hard lines. We would all naturally prefer a system that could give a definitive conclusion about every situation. But such a system does not exist, and we don't need one for responsible action.

We offer the following spectrum to help you determine how abusive a relationship may be.[6] We hope this scale acknowledges

---

6. To be clear, this is *not* a scale to determine whether to take disclosures of abuse seriously, but rather to help you determine the wisest pastoral

the multiple levels of consideration described above, while keeping focus on the essence of abuse.

Generally speaking, the higher the concern is on each of the scales, the greater the urgency. However, not every one of these scales needs to be equally high for responsible action to take place. For instance, a high degree of forcefulness with a relatively low degree of persistence should still be addressed as abuse (e.g., physical assault occurring on a single occasion).

But perhaps more surprisingly, a high degree of persistence with a relatively low degree of forcefulness should also be considered abusive (for example, demeaning or hurtful language occurring consistently over time). In both situations, a person in a position of influence is seeking to limit the personal capacities of another—the first is more immediate control over a person through the acutely painful consequences for their nonconformity; the second is a more gradual control over a person through the chronically painful consequences for their nonconformity.

Similarly, a relatively low degree of diminishing effect on the body may still have a high degree of impact on the soul. A victim may find herself cripplingly insecure, full of self-hate, paralyzed with anxiety, suspicious of any authority, and full of shame as a result of years of withering criticism, threats of abandonment, and constant belittlement. These are ways that one human being can use their God-given personhood to diminish the personhood of another. Such effects on a person are strong indicators of the atmosphere she's been breathing in the home, and reasons for deep concern.

Any disclosure of a person being fearful of someone who is influential over them warrants concern and some degree of careful planning. We begin to lay out how to respond in the next section.

---

action in light of the abuse that has been disclosed. You should take all disclosures of abuse seriously.

Section 2

How to Respond After the Initial Disclosure

You may have picked up this book because you need this information now, in the immediate aftermath of the disclosure or discovery of domestic abuse. While it may be tempting to skip over the material in the first three chapters, we encourage you to read those chapters. They provide important context for what we are discussing in this section, as well as the following section on longer-term ministry.

In a hospital, trauma patients are prioritized based on severity and type of injury. This prioritization is called 'triage'. In domestic abuse care, there is also a priority of care and correction. In the chapters that follow, we will describe how we triage the initial steps of domestic abuse care in the church.

To put it simply, we first care for the victim(s) and do all that we can to ensure their safety. Only after the victim's safety is assured, and with her advice and consent, do we begin working with the person who is acting abusively. Only after those two tasks are well underway can we consider the possibility of a third. If the victim is safe and willing, is healing from the trauma of the abuse, and the abuser is no longer exhibiting abusive patterns and is responding well to ongoing accountability, then efforts at reviving or reconciling the marriage will be much more successful. You must neither get this triage out of order nor fast-track it. The diagram on the following page illustrates this triage.

Victim care

Safety of the victim(s) is paramount.

Listen to her and take her concerns seriously.

Recognize the signs and ask questions.

Report if you suspect harm to children, elderly, or disabled persons.

Assure her of your support.

Assist in practical ways as desired by the victim.

Safety planning with the victim.

Individual counseling as desired by the victim.

Perpetrator correction

Engagement/ Confrontation of the abuser only after safety is established and with victim's advice and consent.

Provide discipleship & accountability if the abuser is open.

Group Intervention Program, if open to it.

Individual counseling if open to it.

Repentance is the goal.

Move more quickly with care and slower with correction.

Marriage reconciliation

Reconciliation to God precedes reconciliation of the marriage.

Reconciliation of the marriage is only recommended when both parties and counselors agree.

The three chapters that make up this section will walk you through what you need to prioritize in the short term.

4

Caring for the Victim

Many live with untold stories, not because they never want to tell them, but because they never encounter safe people and safe places where their stories can be heard.—Wade Mullen[1]

And God heard their groaning, and God remembered his covenant with Abraham, with Isaac, and with Jacob. God saw the people of Israel—and God knew. (Exod. 2:24-25)

Having described the dynamics at play in this situation in the previous chapters, we now want to lay out an action plan. **Wise action in response to domestic abuse always starts with care for the person who is being abused.** The diagram on page 79

---

1. Wade Mullen, *Something's Not Right: Decoding the Hidden Tactics of Abuse and Freeing Yourself From Its Power* (Carol Stream, IL: Tyndale Momentum, 2020), 170.

illustrates how a careful response begins with care for the victim who has approached you with a disclosure of how she is hurting in her home.

You may be wondering why you start with the person being abused instead of the abuser, who is the source of the problem. The main reason is simple: the one who approaches you for help is almost always the person being abused (or a friend on their behalf), not the abuser who often lacks awareness of the problem or its severity. But a second reason is just as compelling: your immediate priority is the safety of the person being abused, not the correction of the abuser. Approaching the abuser first could set off a chain reaction that comes down hard on the spouse under his influence. It's a common mistake among well-meaning church leaders, who often misapply one of two principles: either going to the source to avoid gossip or addressing the head of the home when there's trouble in the home. Both of these are biblical principles. But in order to be robustly biblical, they need to be applied alongside other principles we find in Scripture as the situation necessitates.

The more compelling principles in situations of domestic abuse are those we've shared. Mainly, the deceptive nature of sin and its implications:

1. Darkness will resist exposure to light, so direct confrontation is not always wisest.

2. The self-deceptive nature of sin warps a person's perspective to such an extent that he doesn't see his behavior as abuse.

3. A violent person will do most harm to those who expose him to the least consequences for his actions.

But what if you suspect a darker motivation in the spouse who's claiming to be abused? To put it more frankly, what if you suspect she's exaggerating or even lying? We'd encourage you to consider a few truths, starting with the most basic: You are not God, and therefore have limited access to direct knowledge of what's occurring. This means your instincts are not necessarily an accurate gauge of truth. (And may in fact be conditioned by the nice-guy tactics of an abuser's public persona. As we have said previously, abusive individuals are usually very skilled at impression management.) You are also not a forensic investigator, which means you have neither the authority nor the skills to uncover what goes on behind closed doors in this initial conversation.

Your job is to act responsibly with the level of knowledge you have. And the level of knowledge you have at this point is this: a spouse is disclosing to you that her home hurts. She knows better than you what's going on behind closed doors in her home. She is taking a significant risk by sharing this with you: domestic violence is often under-reported due to fear of retaliation by the abusive spouse. She needs help understanding her situation and responding wisely to it. That's what you know. The impulse to 'get both sides' is the wrong impulse when it comes to an initial response in domestic abuse situations. Both sides will eventually come out. *For now, your focus should be on the immediate safety and welfare of the abused spouse and any children in the home.*[2]

Regarding the spouse accused of abuse, you should not engage him too early in the process. Do not act before the abused spouse has developed a safety plan or apart from her explicit advice and consent. You should address the abusive spouse only when the potential victim is ready for the confrontation. You'll know she's ready when she tells you she's ready as part of the process spelled out below. A good rule of thumb for domestic

---

2. The fear of entertaining a false accusation should not prevent you from listening to a victim and taking her story seriously, just as you would take anyone's story seriously. We recognize that false accusations are possible, though statistically they are not probable, and we offer some guiding principles in Appendix A: FAQs On Domestic Abuse Care when you have concerns about what you are hearing.

abuse response is to move faster with caring for victims, and slower with correcting perpetrators.

What to Do When First Approaching an Abused Spouse

As a church leader, you can be made aware of someone being victimized by spousal abuse in your church in a variety of ways. Sometimes a friend will come to you with direct knowledge of a particular incident. Sometimes a child will disclose it to an adult in the congregation. Sometimes it will be uncovered in marital (or even premarital) counseling. Sometimes, the abused spouse will drop a hint as a fearful cry for help. Regardless, the likelihood of you hearing about it increases as you instill the protection of the family as a value of the community. We say more about this in Chapter 9.

Regardless of how you become aware of a potential situation of domestic abuse, you need to address it safely and responsibly. While every situation is unique, this chapter will give you practical tasks (not necessarily *steps*, since these may not follow a strict sequence) for approaching an abused spouse. In other words, we want you to have a sense of what to do.[3]

We have divided the key tasks you will need to do in approaching a potential victim into *before, during,* and *after* an initial meeting, so you get a sense of the trajectory of care that will continue beyond this meeting.

---

3. By way of reminder, because the vast majority of domestic abuse victims are female, we will use feminine pronouns to refer to victims and the masculine pronouns to refer to abusers. According to the Bureau of Justice Statistics, over 80 percent of criminal IPV victims were female. Shannan Catalano, *Intimate Partner Violence: Attributes of Victimization,* 1993-2011 (Washington DC: U.S. Department of Justice, Office of Justice Programs, Bureau of Justice Statistics, November 2013), 3.

Before Meeting

1. Remind yourself of God's perspective.
Pray for God to help you see this person with His eyes. In the first three chapters, we did our best to present how Scripture gives us God's perspective of abuse and of all the people wrapped up in it. When preparing to meet with someone who is likely being victimized, we encourage you to review these principles. Specifically for meeting with the victim, remember that she is an image bearer who is suffering in a particular way: both her perception and her behaviors are being constrained through the controlling influence of the abuser. Remember, abuse occurs when one spouse uses his capacities to limit the capacities of the other to control her—not just *me before you*, but *me over you*. God hates this and expects those who have strength to do something about it for those who don't.[4]

Can we give a reminder we think is important here? A victim of abuse can often appear either crazier or more critical than the spouse she's accusing of abuse. She may seem scattered, unreasonable, and even defensive. We advise that you suspend judgment for now. If someone has been living under constant abuse, confusion should not be surprising. This is often a normal human response to a distressing situation.

2. Communicate carefully about the meeting.
Communicate discreetly. Generally speaking, use whatever method of communication the abused spouse used with you in her initial disclosure. Be mindful that the abuser likely does not know his spouse is seeking help, and you do not want to be the

---

4. 'Rescue those who are being taken away to death; hold back those who are stumbling to the slaughter. If you say, "Behold, we did not know this," does not he who weighs the heart perceive it? Does not he who keeps watch over your soul know it, and will he not repay man according to his work?' (Prov. 24:11-12, see also Prov. 31:8-9; Jer. 22:3)

one to alert him. If she is communicating to you on the phone, be sensitive to the environment she might be in. If she is using digital means to communicate, encourage her to pay attention to the security of her email address or the device she is using.

Communicate the purpose of the meeting. If the victim has taken the difficult step of disclosing it to you, then the purpose is to understand more fully the situation she is in, guide her understanding of it, and give some direction in it—all outlined in the following tasks. As you reach out to schedule the meeting, you should tell her your intended purpose.

But if the victim has not disclosed the concern, and you became aware of it in a different way—usually through a friend at church—then this initial meeting will have an additional purpose. You will need to help her think through the signs in her marriage that may be indicative of abuse (outlined in the step below). Some silent victims may be trying to cover for the perpetrator out of a sense of duty, fear, or love. Shame about the abuse keeps many from reporting, while others may not be sure if what they are experiencing even constitutes abuse.

If this is the case, then reach out to her accordingly, telling her that you'd like to check in with her in light of what a concerned friend shared. We have found that in most situations, it's best to be upfront with how the concern came to you. This usually means sharing the name of the person, but not apologetically as if that friend did something wrong. Rather, share with confidence that this is the way a community protects the vulnerable among it.

As you reach out to set up a meeting, one last consideration is essential: Consider how her husband's abuse may have sabotaged her perspective of men. She may be unable to avoid fear in the presence of other men, particularly men with the kind of influence church leaders have. If you are a male church leader, you can serve her well as you invite her to a meeting by offering either that she can invite her own trusted friend along or you can ask a caring woman from the church to join. This could be a woman in the church who demonstrates wisdom and grace, ideally who has been entrusted with leadership responsibilities (such as an elder's wife, a female deacon, a ministry coordinator, or a female care advocate).[5] Ask her what she is most comfortable with. It is loving to consider the experience of the victim in how you arrange the composition of the room.

This initial contact is important to get right. Be gentle and compassionate, clearly communicating the purpose of the meeting without over communicating. For example, 'I want you to know my heart was heavy when you told me about what you're going through at home. I want to follow up because your safety is important to me and to the Lord. The purpose of meeting would be to listen to your concerns and help make a plan to keep you safe. We won't take any steps you're not ready for. I just need to have the knowledge necessary to help you.'

It can be incredibly helpful to have the 'caring woman from the church' take the lead in these meetings (under the leadership of the pastoral team, of course). Having a woman appointed to lead the meetings sends a valuable message. It says that the pastors (or male leadership) value the voice and insight of women. This helps victims trust and share. It also is a bit more disarming to have a woman there not merely in presence only, but actually in a leadership role.

---

5. See Appendix E for more direction on serving abuse victims well by training and deploying care advocates in your church. We recommend Called to Peace Ministries (www.calledtopeace.org) for advocacy training.

During the Meeting

3. Assure her that you take her concerns seriously.

Remember, you are an agent of God's love in a tough situation. Exodus 2:23-25, which served as the epigraph for this chapter, provides four helpful verbs that describe God's initial response to the oppression of His people: He *heard* them, He *remembered* His covenant, He *saw* them, and He *knew*. While this passage was not written as a methodology for domestic violence situations, it nevertheless gives insight into how God responded in a situation when His weakened people were being oppressed by those with greater strength. These four verbs, in other words, give us insight into the heart of God toward His people in harm's way.

Open the meeting by assuring her that you take her concerns seriously. You want to hear her story because God hears when His children cry out to Him. You want to see her in her suffering because God does the same for His children. You want to assure her that you will take her seriously and will respond to what she says in a way that will protect and care for her the best you can.

In the case that the victim was not the one to disclose this to you, then you can simply tell her that because you are concerned for her wellbeing, you want to consider if there are concerning indicators in her marriage.

Assure her that safety in the home is not merely *her* concern. It is the Lord's concern. She is probably scared that *she* is the one 'starting something' by speaking up. But domestic abuse is not just her business—it's God's. This assurance is important because, as you'll recall from the previous section, she likely has not felt the freedom to speak up, disagree with anyone, or have an opinion for herself for quite some time. She may be believing that the abuse is her fault or that she is going crazy.

She will likely feel embarrassed and ashamed, anxious and overwhelmed. In fact, her dominant emotion is likely fear.

Begin your meeting by assuring her that you wish to acknowledge her experience, creating an environment where you can help her see a bit more of God's heart toward her situation. For example, 'In this church, we take the health and safety of our people seriously, because the Lord takes it seriously. It may feel scary to share, but I will receive what you say in good faith and do my best to act responsibly with it. I will not mention anything to your husband without your consent and your advice on how to approach him.

I want to ask some questions so that I can better understand what is going on in your home, but please answer them only as you feel comfortable. I'm not asking to be nosy, and your answers are not gossip. It is knowledge that helps us be good stewards of your life before the Lord, not to mention your husband's. Bringing things into the light is always best for people and most glorifying to God.'

4. Ask and listen to her concerns.
Having assured her, you also need to ask into her concerns. Asking the right kind of questions is important, since questions always have statements behind them. Watch your assumptions about her, about him, and about what you would do if it were you. You are simply trying to understand what has occurred. Each individual's experience of abuse is unique, and every case of abuse we've counseled has its own distinct nuances. As the saying goes, 'If you've seen one abusive situation, you've seen one.' Asking good questions takes knowledge, and so we want to provide you with a method for doing that.

It is often helpful to start with specifics and move outward to general patterns. Lenore Walker, a pioneer in the field, suggests asking questions about the first incident of abuse, the most recent incident of abuse, the worst incident of abuse, and a typical incident of abuse.[6] Just let the person in front of you tell the stories. As you listen, do so through the framework of abuse dynamics laid out earlier. Listen specifically for a spouse using his strength to limit her ability to function. This is control, and it increases in its frequency and intensity over time.

To determine the larger patterns, you can move on from hearing these specific accounts to asking more general questions about the relational dynamic that exists between the spouses. This will help you discern patterns.

Leslie Vernick provides a helpful set of questions for discerning larger patterns in the marriage; each of these can be followed up with clarifying *When?*, *Where?*, and *Why?* questions.[7]

- Have you ever been threatened or physically hurt in this relationship?

- Have you ever been an unwilling participant in a sexual act?

- Have you ever felt fearful around your partner?

- Are there times you don't trust your partner's honesty?

- Do you have the freedom to be yourself, make decisions, give your input and say no to things? If not, what happens when you try?

---

6. Lenore Walker, *Abused Women and Survivor Therapy: A Practical Guide for the Psychotherapist* (Washington, DC: American Psychological Association, 1994), 404.

7. Leslie Vernick, 'Three Common Mistakes People Helpers Make When Working with Destructive Marriages,' accessed on July 7, 2018 at https://www.leslievernick.com/wp-content/uploads/2017/09/Three-Common-Mistakes-Workshop-Handout.pdf. She has provided a list of sixty-one similar questions in Vernick, *The Emotionally Destructive Marriage*, 17-25.

- Can you respectfully challenge and confront the attitudes, decisions or behaviors of your partner? When you try, what happens?

Evan Stark suggests the question: 'Is he making you afraid, controlling what you do or say, or making you do something of which you are ashamed?'[8]

The above questions should uncover enough to take responsible action for now. But here are a few more global questions you can ask, if you find them appropriate to where the hurting spouse takes the conversation:

- What happens when you disagree with him or fail to do something he says?

- Have the children been victims of abuse of any kind (verbal, emotional, physical, spiritual)? How frequently does abuse of children occur?

- When he is mad at you or the children, what happens? Are you afraid?

- Does he block you from leaving the room or the house? (This is to get a more specific gauge of the level of violence.)

- Is he willing to take responsibility for his hurtful actions, or does he minimize, blame-shift, tell you that you 'just don't understand' or deny that it happened in the way that you said it happened. (We call this 'crazy-making' or, sometimes, 'gaslighting'. The victim can come to believe that they must be crazy, and this is usually intentionally manipulative behavior on the part of the abuser.)

- Can he hear you when you say these things frighten you? (Does he seem to have genuine empathy for her? Obviously,

---

8. Evan Stark, *Coercive Control: How Men Entrap Women in Personal Life* (New York: Oxford University Press, 2007), 372.

lack of empathy is very concerning and very typical with abusive men.)

- Does he attempt to use his intimidating behavior as a bargaining chip? (Severely manipulative)

- Is he severely verbally abusive? What kinds of things does he say?

- How often are you afraid of the way your husband will respond to provocation or conflict? (When? Where? Why? Under what circumstances?)

- What was the most recent incident of any type of abusive behavior (emotional/verbal/physical/spiritual)? What happened?

- Are there ways he treats you privately that he would never want anyone to know?

- Do you perceive any effects these behaviors are having on you?

- Who else have you told? How have they responded? What was helpful or unhelpful in their responses?

- How safe are you at home currently? As needed, you can follow up with: Do you need a safe place to stay tonight?

- How frequently does this behavior occur?

- How long has this behavior been happening?

- What was the worst incident?

- What is a typical incident?

The answers to the above questions will help you gain a much better picture of the level of oppression in a relationship. If these questions are even being asked, it means that there is some reason for concern about your client's, church member's, group member's, or friend's safety, and perhaps the safety of their children.

5. *Affirm her in her suffering.*

Victims of abuse often doubt their own judgment. They've been told so many times that their feelings are invalid and their choices are wrong, they often lose a sense of clarity. Part of your job in helping them see their situation through God's eyes is bringing moral clarity to what is going on. The Exodus 2 passage mentioned above shows that God's opinion of His people's suffering was that it was indeed suffering—it was wrong, and He was going to do something about it. Such validation occurs regularly in Scripture, because one of the greatest comforts for the people of God in all generations is that God sees their suffering.[9]

Unlike God, you cannot validate the facts being conveyed to you—as we pointed out, you do not have direct knowledge of what occurs behind closed doors. But you act as God does when you affirm that abusive treatment in any form is indeed wrong. It is outside God's design, and therefore has real consequences on spiritual and physical health. Abuse is the opposite of God's design for marital union. And using something outside its design always results in damage, like using fine china as a doorstop. The hurt she feels is the real result of sin done against her—a particularly nefarious kind of sin.

This means you need to avoid the kinds of statements that minimize or dismiss someone's pain. Particularly unhelpful are statements that imply that abuse could be avoided next time with the right response. Here are some examples of invalidating responses to avoid:

---

9. The Psalms are filled with the wonderful truth that the Lord demonstrates concern for the suffering of His people, which leads Him to some form of action. Some of the psalms that address this can be a great comfort to victims who may have lost their confidence that God cares: Psalm 6, 18, 22, 27, 31, 34, 40, 55, 56, and 62.

- 'You shouldn't feel that way.' Or the more subtle, 'I'm sorry you feel that way.'
- 'At least he doesn't...' Or, 'It could be worse.'
- 'Just give your husband what he wants.' Or even worse, 'Just be more submissive.'
- 'What did you do to provoke him?'
- 'Why do you stay if it's really that bad?'

Instead, focus on helping her put her experience into words—summarizing what she has told you and asking if that sounds accurate. For example, 'I hear you saying the way he talks to you is belittling, which makes you angry and embittered. You said he treats you harshly verbally, and occasionally physically? Am I hearing that right?' Try to understand not just *what* information she's conveying, but *how* she's conveying it, asking for feedback to make sure you got it right. 'You seem really overwhelmed. Am I reading you right?' Humbly give her the space to correct your understanding. Let her put the paint where she wants to on the canvas.

6. Help her assess her safety and whether reporting is necessary
Her safety, and the safety of others in the home, is your primary concern in this first conversation. You should ask her about any safety concerns she may have. If the abuse has turned threatening or physical, there may be legitimate concerns about her safety or the safety of others in the home. If children under age 18, disabled individuals, or elderly individuals over the age of 65 are under threat, most states require you to report this to local authorities. You should know if you are a mandatory reporter, and let her know if you believe you have an obligation to report. You can reach out to the National Domestic Violence Hotline (800-799-7233), or to the appropriate domestic violence

agency in your state, for more clarity around this issue, as state laws do vary.[10]

Have on hand the contact information for the national and state resources in Appendix C, and help her understand the different services they offer. She can call local police, who will take a report and intervene if needed. She can call a local or regional domestic violence shelter, which will provide a safe place to go and even advocates who may help them understand their legal options. Also, state governments often connect victims with legal service providers who are willing to offer free legal advocacy. The National Domestic Violence Hotline has advocates available 24/7. You can reach them at thehotline.org or at 1.800.799.SAFE (7233). In addition, some state attorneys

---

10. We are not attorneys, and we encourage you to secure whatever counsel you need to clarify the requirements of your state. Your duty to report, as reflected on the flowchart at the end of this chapter, generally pertains to those whom society believes are unable to protect themselves—that is, children, elderly, or disabled who are suspected to be in danger of abuse, neglect, or exploitation. You will need to consult the laws of your state, but most states have some type of mandatory reporting laws for vulnerable parties.

Often, the spousal victim herself will be reluctant to report the abuse for safety reasons, and she has that right. Because most of the forms of abuse that we are describing in this book are not criminal, reporting for an adult victim can result in greater danger, with no promise of any legal remedies offered. The flowchart at the end of this chapter is intended to help you understand the proper place of reporting—as a first consideration for you regarding secondary vulnerable parties, and as an option for the victim regarding herself. In other words, you care best for a victim not by coercing a self-report, but by offering her resources and choices.

The primary victim's option to report about abuse done to herself should be considered as part of a personal safety plan, alongside other legal options such as restraining orders. If the authorities determine that an actual crime has been committed, the decision to press charges still belongs to the victim, if she is an adult of sound mind. That decision comes at great risk so long as the perpetrator has access to the victim. This is why we suggest that reporting should only be done as part of an established safety plan that removes the victim from access by the abuser.

general have within their office an Office of Victims Advocacy, where victim advocates can answer general questions about the criminal justice process regarding domestic violence, including their rights as crime victims.

But even with being informed of these resources, a victim will often need help understanding that disclosing abuse in the home is the right thing to do. A victim will often feel that coming forward is an act of betrayal to her spouse. But you should show her that disclosure is actually an act of love. Calling abuse what it is may be the best way to love your husband by acting for his good. The Lord defines *good* not as what makes a person most comfortable, but rather what helps him be what God made him to be: a person who loves others, is kind and patient, and in control of himself (Gal. 5:22). Reporting is a necessary part of alerting an abuser to the danger he is in, so that he will not be hardened by sin's deceitfulness (Heb. 3:12-13). Pain is necessary to wake people from their stupor, and should be seen as God's kindness in giving a keen warning (Heb. 12:11). What this means is that sometimes sparing someone from pain is actually unloving. God's worst punishment of a person is not being caught in sin, but rather getting away with it. This is God's 'handing them over' to it (Rom. 3:18-32).

If she remains unwilling, your goal is not to convince her to come forward and/or report. Rather, you are seeking to free her mind of a potential misunderstanding of what is right. You want her to decide for herself what would be the best plan and when to execute it. She may not be ready to 'go public' with her abuse as quickly as you or others are. As the old adage goes, she will be ready when the acid of her pain eats through the wall of her denial. Until then, entrust her timing to the sovereignty of God.

7. Help her make a personal safety plan.

A safety plan is an action strategy to reduce the risk of harm when the threat of abuse increases, often related to the time when established patterns are exposed. Specifically, it details specific action steps the victim will take to protect herself (and her children or any other vulnerable family members) while they remain in the home, in the event that either they decide to leave the home or they find themselves in an emergency. It is vital to have a safety plan in place prior to addressing an abuser. The victim's safety is paramount in the immediate wake of a disclosure of abuse, and throughout the process, and should be the overarching principle guiding every action taken.[11] A safety plan should be created as soon as possible after a disclosure, and modified as necessary throughout the process as circumstances change.[12]

You are helping her create a safety plan for herself that fits her unique situation. Two main benefits come from this: first, a plan makes her safety more likely. But a second less obvious

---

11. Langberg, *Suffering and the Heart of God* (Greensboro, SC: New Growth Press, 2015), 260. See also Cathy Holtmann, 'Calling Women to Safety,' *Responding to Abuse in Christian Homes: A Challenge to Churches and Their Leaders*, ed. Nancy Nason-Clark, Catherine Clark Kroeger, and Barbara Fisher-Townsend (Eugene, OR: Wipf & Stock, 2011), 73.

12. Example safety plan templates can be found in the following resources: Darby Strickland, *Is It Abuse?*, 307-17; Justin and Lindsey Holcomb, *Is It My Fault?*, 187-97; Brenda Branson and Paula J. Silva, *Violence Among Us: Ministry to Families in Crisis*, 119-22; and Brad Hambrick, 'How to Develop a Safety Plan for Domestic Violence,' accessed on July 7, 2018, http://bradhambrick.com/safetyplan/. Also, your community may have trained experts that help create safety plans that could be an excellent resource for this step. For an extra measure of safety, some experienced victim advocates we have consulted suggest starting with the local domestic violence agency in your area in developing a safety plan. They are usually trained in doing lethality assessments and often have more resources at their disposal to help. Appendix C is a good place to get started.

benefit is that you have helped her make a decision on her own. You have begun the process of restoring to her the capacities God designed her to have as one who bears His image.

In terms of the content of the safety plan, it should involve:

- **When she would leave.** Research has consistently demonstrated that a victim's perception of her risk is generally accurate. Help her think through what behaviors from the abuser indicate that she should remove herself from under his influence. (Whenever possible, we encourage the abusive spouse to be the one to leave the home, rather than the victim(s). However, hostile or resistant abusers will often not do that.) If she desires to stay, the safety plan should also include plans for how she will keep herself and any children safe while in the home.

- **Where she would go.** Prearrange a discreet location that is ready to receive her at a moment's notice, like a shelter or the home of a relative or church member. They may need to spend a few days, a few weeks, or even longer outside of the home. Help her think through key family relationships or close friendships who would be willing and able to provide for her.[13]

- **Other logistics.** Help her think through how she will maintain access to her financial resources, what options for legal counsel would she be able to pursue, and what medical care she has available. If the victim has children, a safety plan should include provisions for them, sometimes including pre-packed 'go bag' for each child with a few essentials in case they need to leave the home quickly.

---

13. We recommend having a lethality assessment done. If the situation is extremely dangerous, abusers may stalk friends and family, endangering everyone. In such cases, it is wise to find a location that the abuser doesn't know. We also discuss lethality and risk assessments more in Chapter 8.

It is well known that leaving the home is the most dangerous time for an abuse victim. Justin and Lindsey Holcomb observe that over 75 percent of separated women suffer post-separation abuse. Approximately 75 percent of all domestic homicides occur while the victim is trying to leave their abuser or has just left the relationship.[14] A safety plan can help mitigate the danger of this courageous and difficult decision.

8. Plan follow up.

This person just shared quite a bit with you, and she should know that this is not the end of her care. You should at least mention follow up care options, if not get something tentatively scheduled. This is an appropriate time to introduce the idea that her ongoing care will need to extend beyond just you. Her situation demands more than one person can offer, and God built His church to be a body with many parts.

You can offer to arrange any number of ways the church can serve her.

- Pastoral or lay care, with caregivers trained in the dynamics of relational abuse. Our hope is that this book will be a help in training those in the church who are helping to provide care for victims of abuse.

- A mentoring relationship, ideally with a wise person who has survived abuse.

- Discreet conversations with members who specialize and are trained in different areas of practical need: finances, legal issues, career guidance.

You should also make her aware of community resources that may be a helpful part of her ongoing care, including:

---

14. Justin S. and Lindsey A. Holcomb, *Is It My Fault? Hope and Healing for Those Suffering Domestic Violence.* (Chicago: Moody, 2014), 65.

- Local professional counselors who specialize in domestic abuse or trauma.

- Domestic abuse agencies and shelters that specialize in helping victims know their options, manage the case, and even help with self-sufficiency planning. We hope that Appendix C will at least provide you a starting point to help with resourcing. We encourage you to familiarize yourself with your local counselors, agencies, advocates, and shelters so that you will be prepared when the need arises.

When you give the victims options for assistance, ask what would be most helpful rather than insist on any one thing. It might be tempting to think that insisting on a certain kind of help is the best way to show concern for a person. But for someone who has been controlled and belittled for many years, this kind of well-intentioned gesture may reinforce the sense that she's unable to make good personal decisions for herself. It is important when working with abuse victims to constantly bear in mind the power imbalance that has reordered this person's relational world for years, and to do everything they can to assist the domestic violence victim in making her own decisions.

Also important to note here is that marriage counseling—even if the victim asks for it—is not advisable in the early stages of uncovering domestic abuse. It is too easy for an intelligent abuser to use it for his advantage by painting a certain picture of the wife when in counseling, and using his personal interpretation of the counselor's advice to maintain control over her.

After Meeting

9. Follow up as planned.

Coordinate discreetly with key helpers, then follow up. Plan it into your schedule early, so that you can retain the margin necessary for a demanding situation like this. But also, by using other helpers, you don't allow this situation to dominate your own. Our point here is simply that you are not being invasive by checking back in; rather, you are showing her that your care is ongoing. Often victims of abuse will allow the situation to linger a long time before they choose to take action. You need to show her a proper balance of patience and presence.

You will also want to clarify *if, when,* and *how* she would like for the church to engage her abuser. Do not engage him before she is ready; and do not engage him without her advice on timing. She knows him better than you do.

Concluding Thoughts

This conversation is a difficult one, but it may be the ray of light that reminds a hurting spouse what is on the other side of those clouds. She's lived under them for so long, she may have forgotten what light is like. She may not remember what a gentle conversation feels like, or the confidence that comes from moral clarity, or the security of believing that God's love is an active power in her life.

You are preparing to have a conversation that feels high-risk and high-stakes. That's because it is indeed both. But remember, the Lord is with you as you seek to be an agent of His love in a difficult situation.

Additional Resources for Victims and Caregivers

Branson, Brenda, and Paula J. Silva. *Violence among Us: Ministry to Families in Crisis.* (Valley Forge, PA: Judson Press, 2007). (For caregivers)

Forrest, Joy. *Called to Peace: A Survivor's Guide to Finding Peace and Healing After Domestic Abuse.* (Raleigh, NC: Blue Ink Press, 2018). (For caregivers and victims) Her book also has a companion workbook, designed to serve as a gospel-based support group curriculum. Joy's ministry, also named Called to Peace, serves victims and trains advocates. www.calledtopeace. org

Hambrick, Brad. 'How to Develop a Safety Plan for Domestic Violence.' Accessed January 24, 2021. http://bradhambrick. com/safetyplan/. (For caregivers and victims)

Holcomb, Justin S., and Lindsey A. Holcomb. *Is It My Fault? Hope and Healing for Those Suffering Domestic Violence.* (Chicago: Moody, 2014). (For victims)

Jackson, Tim, and Jeff Olson. *When Violence Comes Home: Help for Victims of Spouse Abuse.* (Grand Rapids: RBC Ministries, 2002). E-book. (For victims)

Strickland, Darby A. *Domestic Abuse: Recognize, Respond, Rescue* (Resources for Changing Lives). (Phillipsburg, NJ: P&R Publishing, 2018). (For caregivers)

Strickland, Darby A. *Domestic Abuse: Help for the Sufferer* (Resources for Changing Lives). (Phillipsburg, NJ: P&R Publishing, 2018). (For victims)

Strickland, Darby A. *Is It Abuse: A Biblical Guide to Identifying Domestic Abuse and Helping Victims.* (Phillipsburg, NJ: P&R Publishing, 2020). (For caregivers and victims)

Tracy, Steven R. *Mending the Soul: Understanding and Healing Abuse.* (Grand Rapids, MI: Zondervan, 2008). (For victims and caregivers) There is also a *Mending the Soul Workbook* for use in facilitating support groups for victims. Mending the Soul also trains caregivers to facilitate support groups at www.mendingthesoul.org.

Vernick, Leslie. *How to Act Right When Your Spouse Acts Wrong.* (Colorado Springs: Waterbrook Press, 2001). (For victims)

Vernick, Leslie. *The Emotionally Destructive Marriage.* (Colorado Springs: WaterBrook, 2013). (For victims)

Domestic Violence Victim Disclosure Flowchart

We know that responding to a victim's disclosure of domestic violence cannot be reduced to a flowchart. The sinful impulse to prioritize processes over people adds insult to injury. But domestic abuse disclosures involve important and complex dynamics that cannot be missed. This flowchart is our effort to lay out in logical order the most critical responses, in the hope that it will help you love people well in the midst of a chaotic and confusing situation.

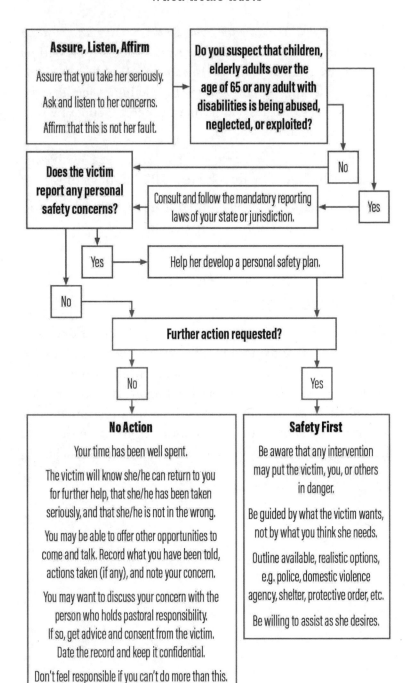

Assure, Listen, Affirm

Assure that you take her seriously.

Ask and listen to her concerns.

Affirm that this is not her fault.

Do you suspect that children, elderly adults over the age of 65 or any adult with disabilities is being abused, neglected, or exploited?

No

Yes

Does the victim report any personal safety concerns?

Consult and follow the mandatory reporting laws of your state or jurisdiction.

Yes → Help her develop a personal safety plan.

No

Further action requested?

No

Yes

No Action

Your time has been well spent.

The victim will know she/he can return to you for further help, that she/he has been taken seriously, and that she/he is not in the wrong.

You may be able to offer other opportunities to come and talk. Record what you have been told, actions taken (if any), and note your concern.

You may want to discuss your concern with the person who holds pastoral responsibility. If so, get advice and consent from the victim. Date the record and keep it confidential.

Don't feel responsible if you can't do more than this.

Safety First

Be aware that any intervention may put the victim, you, or others in danger.

Be guided by what the victim wants, not by what you think she needs.

Outline available, realistic options, e.g. police, domestic violence agency, shelter, protective order, etc.

Be willing to assist as she desires.

5

Confronting the Abuser

All the perpetrator asks is that the bystander do nothing. He appeals to the universal desire to see, hear and speak no evil.
—Judith Herman[1]

Declare these things; exhort and rebuke with all authority. Let no one disregard you. (Titus 2:15)

We urge you not to take action on anything in this chapter until you have taken the proper actions from the previous chapter, especially a safety plan for the victim. The impulse to either 'get the other side of the story' or to 'sit him down and teach him the right way to treat a woman' can cause more harm

---

1. Judith Herman, *Trauma and Recovery: The Aftermath of Violence— From Domestic Abuse to Political Terror* (New York: Basic Books, 1997), 7.

through premature action. Only when a safety plan is in place, and only with the advice and consent of the victim, can you begin to engage the abusive spouse wisely.

What to Do When First Approaching an Abusive Spouse

But we also want to help orient you to this next task in the process of correcting an abuser. To do so, we will begin by helping you discern two ditches you want to avoid as you take the next few steps down this difficult path.

The first ditch is cynicism. After hearing what a victim of abuse has told you about this man, you may be tempted to despise him. The outrage that may have welled up inside you can taint the way you treat him. But we must remember that abusers, just like victims, are created in the image of God and have inherent value, worth, and dignity. You are not speaking to a monster, but to a man created to be like God whose corrupted perceptions and behaviors, as described in Chapter 2, are causing harm to those he loves. Remember, you are an agent of God's love. And correction is an act that benefits him at personal cost to you.

The second ditch is naivete. As a church leader, your first impulse is probably to be generous in giving the benefit of the doubt to people you speak to. This is a general application of the wisdom of Proverbs 18:17, 'The one who states his case first seems right, until the other comes and examines him.' You will definitely find there are two sides to every story while working with cases of domestic abuse. In fact, the abuser's story can often end up sounding quite different and more believable than the one you heard from the victim. He may even portray himself as the victim of her manipulation. This is to be expected, and we would encourage you, in light of what we've established about the dynamics of abuse, to arm yourself with a healthy realism.

As you prepare to meet with an abuser, we encourage you to ask the Lord to grant you eyes to see what the victim, who knows him best and most intimately, has seen. Too often, the principle of Proverbs 18:17 is misused to justify leaders simply going along with who they personally find most believable. The problem is, who they find most believable is often the one who is most skilled in representing his perspective. But simply believing the most persuasive person can unwittingly violate another principle, this one from Proverbs 26:24-26:

> Whoever hates disguises himself with his lips
> and harbors deceit in his heart;
>   when he speaks graciously, believe him not,
> for there are seven abominations in his heart;
>   though his hatred be covered with deception,
> his wickedness will be exposed in the assembly.

Christian ministry requires Christian realism. We cannot equate pastoral kindness with *nice guy* sentiments. Solomon warned of people who speak graciously, but disguise the destructive orientation of their heart. Where is this deceit eventually exposed? *In the assembly.* You are beginning a corrective process on behalf of God's people, a community assembled for mutual accountability under the Word of God. This does not mean you will magically unveil the particularities of the situation in an instant. But it does mean that the truth will be incrementally revealed in the context of the relationships you will be helping to assemble. The process will help reveal the truth.

And that process guards church leaders from committing the error of partiality. Proverbs 18:5 says, 'It is not good to be partial to the wicked or to deprive the righteous of justice.' Partiality is our tendency to go with what we're most impressed with, what we're most comfortable with, or what provides the quickest and easiest explanation. In other words, we all tend to prefer the narrative that is least personally disruptive. The advantage of this lies with an abuser, who is benefited by maintaining the status quo. Thus, partiality can lead to injustice for those God wants to protect. This is why a solid process is so important in protecting God's people.

As in the previous chapter, we have described the key tasks you will need to do in approaching an abuser *before, during,* and *after* an initial meeting, so you get a sense of the trajectory of correction that will continue beyond this meeting.

Before Meeting

1. Remind yourself of God's perspective of the abuser.
Pray for God to help you see this person through His eyes. We encourage you to review Section 1 to understand God's perspective on abuse and the abuser. Remember, he is a marred image-bearer, whose sin manifests itself in specific ways. Both his perception and his behavior are corrupted by a variety of factors, such as entitlement, objectification, control, deception (of self or others), shame, false beliefs (about God, self, or others), past hurts (such as abuse, abandonment, or loss), and even mental health issues. In this way, abuse is a double-desecration of the image of God—one image-bearer using his power to exert control over another to get what he wants at her expense. Not just *me before you*, but *me over you*. God hates this and expects those who have strength to do something about it for those who don't. Psalm 11:5 says, 'The Lord tests the righteous, but his soul hates the wicked and the one who loves violence.'

Like the initial conversation with the victim, this one is also a high-risk, high-stakes conversation. But remember, the Lord is with you as you seek to be an agent of His love in a difficult situation.

2. Obtain the explicit advice and consent of the victim about everything you will discuss.

As we've tried to make clear, caring well for an adult victim of abuse means respecting her agency and allowing her to choose how best to move forward. Seeking both her advice and her consent is vital to helping her make this choice.

In terms of advice, you are seeking her insights into the particular dynamics of her abusive relationship. She knows the abuser better than anyone, what is most likely to trigger him, or what is more likely to create a volatile and dangerous situation. Her advice will be vital for determining the right timing and the right angle for the conversation.

In terms of consent, you must realize that your having a conversation with her abuser could make her life much harder in the short-term. Even if the abuser were to lash out at you in anger in that meeting, you will likely not pay the harshest consequences of this confrontation. The greatest hurt will likely be reserved for those in his own home. Even if the couple is separated, he can still retaliate against her in a variety of ways, including taking it out on the kids, stalking her whereabouts, or harassing her through texts and phone calls. Because she will face these potential threats, she should be able to mitigate them by agreeing to the *timing* and the *content* of your engagement with him.

Regarding content, you will need to provide to the abuser some reason for the confrontation. Get the victim's permission for what details that reason should include. For example, you might say: 'Pastor David and I are planning to tell him that we've heard about his use of threats and his demeaning words, as well as him punching that hole in the wall. Is that okay with you?' She might say that is fine with her; or she may prefer you only bring up the threats and demeaning words for now, but not mention the hole in the wall. Given that your top priority is the safety of the victim, and she has a better sense for what would put her in danger, you should withhold the detail about the wall for now. You can always ask the simple question, 'What things that we have discussed are okay to bring up in this meeting, and what things would you rather we not bring up at this time?'

Regarding timing, you will need to be as specific as possible. For example, 'Pastor David and I are available to speak with your husband on Thursday evening. Does that time slot allow you to act on your safety plan if needed?' Listen to the various factors she brings up—she knows the rhythm of the home. No time will be ideal. You are usually trying to find the least disruptive time.

See the flowchart at the end of this chapter for an at-a-glance guide to help you discern what to do in your situation.

3. Plan a meeting that includes at least one elder/pastor who understands the dynamics of relational abuse.[2]
The composition of the room is important in this meeting, too. This meeting is setting a corrective trajectory, and pastoral presence is vital. The pastors are responsible to lead the church

---

2. Knowledge of and some experience with the dynamics of relational abuse is extremely important in pastoral care/correction meetings of this type. This book is a start on basic knowledge, but there is no substitute for experience. If you do not have pastors with training and experience in this area, we would encourage you to consult with someone, ask a trained advocate for help, or consult with your local DV agency. Chris Moles offers training and coaching specifically related to perpetrator care and correction through chrismoles.org. Joy Forrest offers victim advocate training and a church partnership program through calledtopeace.org. There are qualified and experienced people who want to help you care well. Utilize them.

through the discipline process, and discipline in domestic violence situations is particularly complex. As we have said, it is also critical that all those involved in the process understand the elements of abuse that we have described in Section 1. We will lay out what to communicate to an abuser about accountability during the meeting below.

For now, as you plan a meeting, we simply want to make clear that the meeting you're about to have is part of a larger process of church discipline. You may or may not choose to use this language initially, given the tendency to equate *church discipline* with *excommunication,* which in actuality is only the final step in the careful, measured process of church discipline. But early on, church discipline is simply Christians drawing attention to areas of a fellow member's life that are displeasing to the Lord. The point you want to emphasize in this initial meeting is that private sins among God's people are a community concern (Matt. 18:15-20; 1 Cor. 5:1-5; Eph. 5:7-14). This is why at least two people should be present, with at least one of them being a pastor or elder of the church.

An additional advantage of multiple people in the meeting is the shared capacity to remember important details, to take notes, and to contribute insights from shared convictions in the meeting.

Another person that may be helpful to have in the room is a church friend of the abuser. While this may not be helpful in every situation, some advantages of having an advocate in the room for the person accused of abuse include: You go the extra mile to display a type of leadership that is not forceful or threatening, and you get to communicate directly to a friend he'd be talking to anyway. In addition, it makes reaching out to set up a meeting a bit easier.

In terms of reaching out, when you ask the victim if you can reach out, you can also seek their advice on the best way to reach out. 'What's the best way for me to ask him to meet? What timing serves you best for me contacting him?' You also want to tell her what you plan to say.

Generally, we advise you to use the most personal form of communication (e.g., phone rather than email or text) and then to be direct about your reason for meeting, without being detailed: 'I would like to meet with you to discuss (whatever you and the spouse have decided would be the best way to express the concern). Can you meet Pastor David and me tomorrow after work?' Also, 'If you are more comfortable having a friend from the church join us too, we'd welcome that.'

Sometimes a person will push back with questions, other times he will simply agree to meet. If there are questions, politely refer to the meeting as the place to talk everything through.

During the Meeting

4. Explain to him that you take the victim's concerns seriously.
Thank him for coming and acknowledge that he probably has many questions. Assure him that you want to help make everything clear, and that you need the Lord's help to do so. Then pray to begin the meeting. We advise a brief prayer that focuses on the need for the Lord to give wisdom, and for our need to be receptive (Prov. 2:6; 28:26, James 1:5).

After praying, move directly to stating your concern about what his spouse has shared is happening at home, **sharing only what the victim has given you explicit permission to share.** He has likely already heard these concerns from his spouse, so your purpose is not so much to inform him, but to weigh in with biblical acknowledgment that such behavior is indeed concerning. It's best to offer a general concern paired with a specific example.

'I asked for this meeting because I wanted to show you the respect of speaking directly to you. Your wife has shared concerns about your conduct toward her, and I need you to know that Scripture tells me to take her concerns seriously.

'Let me share some specific concerns she gave me permission to convey to you [we are providing a more-direct approach and a less-direct approach for each]:

1. *She says you often put her down and demean her with words like "..." and "..." when you're angry. [Or a less-direct approach utilizing a question, "Are hurtful words sometimes used in your interactions with her?" "Can you give me some examples?"]*

2. *She says you control the money. She has no access to the bank accounts and is often confused about why you blow up about purchases she makes. [Or, again less directly, "She mentioned something about the finances. Is there mutuality and reciprocity in the stewarding of your money?"]*

3. *She says you are physically aggressive to her. You shoved her into a doorframe last Friday evening. [Or, "She said something about an incident last Friday. Can you tell me more about that?"][3]*

He will likely not need to be prompted for a response to these accusations. If he is silent, you can simply ask, 'How do you respond to these concerns?' Whether prompted or unprompted,

---

3. It cannot be stressed often or strongly enough that you should have vetted each of these concerns (and the way that you intend to word them) with the spouse, PRIOR to meeting with the husband and bringing them up. Bringing up any one of these things with him *could* increase the danger to her, particularly if they are not separated. That doesn't mean that you shouldn't bring them up. Only that you should have followed our suggestion to get the victim's explicit consent and advice about any conversations that you have with him, particularly if you are bringing up new things, if it is early in the process, or if the couple is not separated.

he may respond in a variety of ways. He may own these concerns, but as isolated occurrences, not as a part of an overall pattern of behavior as the victim has probably described it. Or he may minimize them, admitting they are unpleasant, but not nearly as alarming as his wife indicated. Or he may blame the spouse for provoking his response through how difficult she was being. Minimizing, denying, and blaming are the abusive person's stock-in-trade. Since these responses have worked with her, he may now try them on you.

- Minimizing: 'I'm not demeaning her. I was only joking.' (Prov. 26:18-19)

- Denying: 'I am not financially controlling. She's lying.' (Prov. 28:13-14)

- Blaming: 'I only shoved her when she refused to get out of my way.' (Gen. 3:12-13)

His story will not line up with hers in some significant way. In the moment, you may be tempted to back off the concern because he is providing a reasonable explanation. But here's a good theological reminder at this point: You are not God, and thus don't have the capacity to know directly what is going on. Your job is to be responsible with the knowledge you've been given. The knowledge you've been given is that a person in a vulnerable position has described her situation as threatening. Your job is to take seriously her concern and make accountability clear.

In short, you need to be clear to the person in front of you that you are taking his spouse's concerns seriously because this is what pleases God in a world of misused authority.[4] Being

---

4. We have already mentioned Jesus' clear insistence that authority must not be misused among His people in Mark 11:42-45. But you can also look to the example of the apostles defending the church from those who deceive, manipulate, and muscle the church into error, rather than demonstrate the gentle, patient love of the true apostles. Consider the

clear on this will require you to insist that his spouse is telling you that she sees *patterns* of behavior, not isolated instances of sin. As you do this, you are being vigilant for these classic defensive postures.

5. Ask and listen to his concerns.
It is also appropriate in this meeting to ask him if he has any concerns. Your purpose is not to create a hostile *he said, she said* dynamic, but rather to gain insight into his perspective of what is happening here. Ask about his perspective of their marriage, of his wife, and of his own role in the relationship. Just as the victim has a story, the abuser also has a story. Let him tell it. It is a way of showing honor to him as the image of God, of gaining trust, and of establishing a base of knowledge for how he thinks and reacts. He will share more about himself and his backstory. This will all be helpful in discerning a knowledgeable way forward that protects the victim and handles a potential abuser with fairness.

> *'Obviously, each story has a few sides. I'd love to hear your thoughts on why your wife expressed these concerns to me. Or how your marriage got to the point it has. Or what is hard for you about this conversation.'*
>
> *Employ active-listening responses such as 'tell me more about that,' 'give me an example,' 'help me understand,' or 'what do you mean?' Ask open-ended questions rather than ones that can be answered with a word. The 5 Ws and 1 H of good information gathering will serve you well here: who, what, when, where, why, and how.*

contrast in Paul's disposition between the deceivers threatening the church in Galatians 5:7-12 and immature believers in need of growth in 1 Thessalonians 2:7-12.

6. Clarify how Scripture talks about abuse and how your church responds appropriately.

Using the word 'abuse' will escalate the conversation. That doesn't necessarily mean you should avoid it entirely, since it is an effective way of showing the moral urgency of his spouse's concerns. But *how* you use it is very important.

Generally speaking, it's a good strategy to broach the topic by simply naming the behaviors that his spouse has already named. As you identify them specifically, you can eventually get the point of characterizing those behaviors as 'destructive,' 'hurtful,' 'harmful,' 'manipulative,' 'harsh,' 'mean,' 'controlling,' or 'abusive.' The language you use should correlate with the level of clarity you have from the victim's description. You would likely call a slap across the face as 'abusive,' but you might call cutting up his wife's credit cards, 'controlling.' The former is immediately clear as abusive, the latter would need further information about the larger patterns of interaction that characterize the marriage. However, we know from Scripture that God is displeased with a husband behaving in any of these ways toward his family. Don't get into arguments over words with a husband at this point. As long as you are describing behaviors that are inconsistent with loving her as Christ loves the church, you are having a worthwhile conversation. As patterns of behavior become clear, as you begin to see and show him (if he has eyes to see) the *me over you* patterns of behavior that we described in Section 1 (and this may be long past your initial conversation with him), you will be able to apply the word 'abuse' more credibly.

Approaching it this way allows you to address the global issue of abuse, what it is and what it is not. It may be helpful for you to review Section 1 as you prepare for this meeting, and other meetings with this man. Abuse is one spouse relating to another in a way that uses his personal capacities to diminish her ability to live according to God's design, making her easier to control so that he gets his way. It is *me over you* behavior. It is the desecration of God's image, a dark opposite to love that builds up, and an ungodly misuse of authority. And the hardest thing about explaining abuse in the context of this conversation is that an abuser usually doesn't see it himself.

When you do get around to applying the term 'abuse' to his behavior, whether in this meeting or a later one, you might say something like 'You're probably wondering why I'm this alarmed about your wife's concerns. I'm about to use a word you may not like and may never have considered, so I want to be clear what I mean and what I don't mean. The word is "abuse."

'What I don't mean by "abuse" is anything your wife doesn't like about the way you treat her. No one should use the word "abuse" as a generic catch-all for anything mean or unpleasant. If that's how we used it, then almost anything could be described as abuse.

'Instead, I'm trying to see abuse from God's eyes. In other words, what does He consider abusive? Let me share some things I've learned about abuse, so that you understand why I'm concerned...'

Then you would describe the dynamics of abuse that we described in Section 1. This would also be an appropriate place to explain your church's domestic abuse policy, if you have one.[5]

The person in front of you will likely respond somewhere on the following continuum, ranging from hostility to openness. Even as we lay out this spectrum, keep in mind that an initial

---

5. In this book, we lay out a protocol for intervention, but each church should develop for itself the appropriate position statements, policies, and protocols for responding to domestic abuse situations. Appendix D explains how to develop a domestic abuse policy for your organization and provides a sample policy.

Hostile	Reluctance or Resistance	Open
This person exhibits the same destructive behavior towards you that he exhibits towards his spouse.	This person demonstrates reluctance (passive) or resistance (active) to change. He's not abusive towards you. He just thinks you're wrong.	This person appears open to change, at least initially. He exhibits a willingness to see and own his abuse.

reaction is never a complete one, for good or bad. Still, wherever he lands on this continuum will likely dictate the next few steps. We will go over this in more detail in Chapter 8.

- **Hostile**—He responds with something like, 'That's definitely not me! How dare you!' He may actually even exhibit the same abusive, destructive, harsh behaviors toward you that he exhibits toward her. You may get a front-row seat to her reality.

- **Reluctant or Resistant**—His response may be closer to, 'That's not me. Here is what is actually happening,' Or, 'That's not me, but I will go through your process.' He isn't abusive toward you. He just either passively (reluctant) or actively (resistant) thinks you're wrong.

- **Open**—He may say, 'I don't think that's me, but let me think about it more.' Or he may agree, at least partially, to what his wife is saying. He appears, at least initially, open to change and to see and own his abuse.

However he reacts, you have an opportunity to model a Christ-like response. Don't return a hostile response with aggression, or an open one with an assumption of repentance. Regardless of where he falls on this spectrum, he will likely make same reference to his own intentions—'I would never intentionally hurt her,' 'I can honestly say I've never meant to do her harm,' or 'Who are you to judge my intentions?' It's helpful to be prepared with the robust doctrines of sin and of humanity we laid out in Chapter 2, emphasizing that Scripture makes it clear that our intentions are often not clear to us because of the self-deceit of sin. We need community, the Holy Spirit, the Word of God, etc. to help us discern our true motives.

7. Set clear short term expectations.
In this initial meeting with a perpetrator of abuse, you want to set clear expectations for him. The main goal of these expectations is *accountability for change.* Such accountability aids in both protection for the victim and, if the Lord wills, repentance for the abuser. The expectations you are setting in this meeting are short-term expectations. You cannot set long-term expectations until you see the initial fallout of these initial conversations.

In the short term, the individual's repentance before God is of greater priority than reconciliation in the marriage. Without brokenness before God, the marriage remains unsafe for the abused spouse.[6] Even when a man is owning his guilt for abuse, you cannot tell the difference between godly sorrow and worldly sorrow in the short term. Only the establishment of new patterns of righteousness can reliably demonstrate godly sorrow (2 Cor. 7:10-13). That takes time.

So in the short term, set these expectations for him:

- 'We do not recommend marriage counseling at this time.' Abuse is not a couples' issue, since it is not the behavior of the spouse that provokes abuse. The work that needs to be done is focused on the abuser.

---

6. See Section 3 on How to Care in the Long Term for guidance on reconciliation in an abusive marriage.

- 'We expect all abusive behaviors to stop immediately.' Behavioral change is expected immediately, even before the possibility of genuine heart change. This may seem counterintuitive to biblical counselors used to focusing on the heart, but it is nevertheless consistent with a biblical approach. The abuse, as it has been described in this meeting, must stop immediately.

- 'You need help, and that help will not be comfortable for you.' Make clear to him that he does not have the resources on his own to see what he needs to see or to change what he needs to change. He needs the exhortation of other Christians to avoid being further hardened by the deceitfulness of sin (Heb. 3:12-13). He also benefits from community resources that shed light on just how distressing domestic abuse is in other families. We will say more on this in the next step.

- 'After this meeting, if you shame, threaten, or otherwise manipulate your wife, we will consider that abusive behavior.' Making this clear is important for the safety of the victim, who has to live with this man (unless, of course, the situation has already warranted the safety plan to be initiated).

NOTE: If the victim has determined she wants to separate for her own safety, then you may need to inform the abusive spouse in this meeting. You should be clear on your theological position on separation, divorce, and reunification in cases of abuse. We have tried to provide you some guidance in Appendix B to help you with this. While we cannot respond for you, we believe that Scripture compels Christians to stand on the side of the oppressed. Thus, we would probably tell him that we support his spouse's decision to separate in the hopes that this accountability will wake him up to his sin. He will likely want to know how long the separation or the overall process will be. It's best to be straightforward that it will be longer than he wants. Months or years instead of weeks or days. This will help him realize early that he will not be able to rush the process. We encourage perpetrators to be patient with the process and to take a long-term perspective: 'We realize this might seem like an impossibly long period of time. But if the Lord is gracious and grants you decades of sweet, abuse-free marriage, you will agree that this is more than worth it.' You may also want to compare this timeframe to the number of years the marriage has been abusive.

8. Help him make a personal accountability plan.

Just like the usual outcome of a first session with a victim is a personal safety plan, the usual outcome of a first session with an abuser is a personal accountability plan. The point of this plan is to clearly define what an abuser must commit to. In summary, he is committing to: no abuse, accountability, individual counseling, and pastoral oversight. This personal accountability plan sets the trajectory for future care.

The content of the personal accountability plan will certainly vary by situation, but generally includes:

- **No abuse.** This plan involves zero tolerance of future abuse. If abusive behavior occurs, those caring for the victim will support her in whatever next steps are outlined in her safety plan. Further abusive action will also advance the process of church discipline.

- **Accountability.** We usually recommend an accountability team of three to four people who know the individual well and are already involved in his life. We also recommend that at least one of those people be a trained member of your domestic abuse care team. We usually call these people care advocates. (See Appendix E for a sample care advocate role description.) Work with him to determine who would be best, but they must be people who possess godly character and some level of biblical knowledge and understanding of the dynamics of abuse, as discussed in this book.

For accountability to work, it must be regular and all parties should be communicating in some form regularly. Ideally, a husband seeking to free himself from abuse should have a weekly meeting with at least a portion of the team, and the team should be regularly communicating privately.

- **Individual counseling.** We recommend that you maintain a referral list of Christ-centered counselors with training and experience in domestic abuse. Whether they are lay or professional counselors, the ideal is that they have a robust understanding of both Scripture and of the dynamics involved in domestic abuse.

However, you may not have that luxury in your area. If that is the case, be assured that your church can maintain an overall scope of care that is Christ-centered while making use of a counselor who may not approach things from a biblical framework but has training and experience working with perpetrators of domestic abuse. The expertise he brings on the common factors involved in domestic violence is important for keeping families safe.

Part of counseling is growing in the awareness of what constitutes abuse. A good counselor will measure progress in part by the steps a counselee takes to learn about the specific dynamics of abusive behavior, so that he might better discern his own. There are a few ways to do this. One way is to provide reading material on domestic abuse. We recommend several resources in this book. But just reading will have limited effect. Reading that compels self-reflection is far more likely to yield change. This is why ongoing conversations, and perhaps some journaling in between to aid those conversations, is vital.

Another (and more experientially powerful) way of educating involves external resources. Many communities have local resources such as state domestic abuse agencies or local batterer intervention and prevention programs (BIPPs). These are educational groups, usually facilitated by a local domestic violence agency (see Appendix C). These programs will not address the heart, as only God's Word can; however, they can provide firsthand knowledge of just how ugly and destructive abuse is. Many men have *am I like that guy?* moments of clarity.

- **Pastoral Care.** Whatever the counseling option, it's your job as a church leader to help the abuser process what he's hearing from a biblical framework, or see to it that a biblically competent person does.

  To allow for this, you should *suggest* (you cannot demand) that the abuser sign a release of information with his counselor so that his counselor can talk to individuals from the church who serve on the abuser's care team. It is also typically advisable that the abuser's counselor also has a release of information and open dialogue with the victim's counselor. We will explore this more in Chapter 8 on long-term care.

  The goal of pastoral care is to move him toward Christ Jesus, who alone can change his heart. The grace of God in Jesus Christ should be the driving force behind this care. A mature understanding of grace will insist that it brings about *both* forgiveness *and* discipline away from ungodly conduct (Titus 2:11).

  Practically speaking, you will want to define very specifically what ongoing care will look like moving forward. How often will you (or someone else from the care team) be able to meet with him? What kind of access will he have to you? How will communication happen (call, text, email)?

The content of those meetings will largely be overseeing the other parts of the accountability plan, as described above.

At the end of the meeting, leave him with a word of hope. The very fact that you worked through an accountability plan is an act of hope. Pray with him, and depending on your read in the moment, you may even ask him to pray.

After Meeting

9. *Follow up with both the victim and the abuser.*
Knowing that you are meeting with her abuser, the victim will likely be extremely nervous about this meeting. So don't delay in getting back with her. Reach back out to her to let her know how the meeting went and how he is being held accountable. During this follow-up conversation with her, you will want to be particularly attentive to and empathize with how she is feeling about your description of how the meeting went.

- Is she concerned about further abuse? Have her safety concerns significantly increased after this meeting?

- How is she feeling about the personal accountability plan that you developed with her spouse? Does she have any concerns about any aspect of his personal accountability plan? Does her personal safety plan need to be re-evaluated?

Of course, you will also want to follow-up with him and with his accountability team. If you have agreed to weekly meetings with him, make sure to get those scheduled. If you owe him a BIPP or individual counselor referral, do the necessary research to help him find the best help he can get. Please consult the resources in Appendix C to get pointed in the right direction.

Concluding Thoughts

The conversation outlined in this chapter is a hard one. You may be the first person outside his family to confront him about his abuse. But this is what it is to be an agent of God's love, bringing clarity to a murky situation.

You are modeling for this man a heart that shares God's concern for his family and for him. If he responds aggressively, he is only acting in accordance with the pattern you saw. If he responds brokenly, then be encouraged that at least a ray of the Spirit's light is visible. If he responds halfway, be assured that this is probably most common, and don't burden yourself with the expectation of being able to predict which direction he'll head. Time will tell.

If the Lord grants repentance, he will one day see this conversation for what it is: your humble attempt to practice James 5:19-20, 'My brothers, if anyone among you wanders from the truth and someone brings him back, let him know that whoever brings back a sinner from his wandering will save his soul from death and will cover a multitude of sins.'

Additional Resources for Perpetrators and Caregivers

Bancroft, Lundy. *Why Does He Do That? Inside the Minds of Angry and Controlling Men* (New York: G.P. Putnam's Sons, 2002). (For caregivers)

Bancroft, Lundy. 'Guide for Men Who Are Serious About Changing—Part 1' and 'Guide for Men Who Are Serious

About Changing—Part 2,' https://lundybancroft.com/articles/guide-for-men-who-are-serious-about-changing-part-1/ and https://lundybancroft.com/articles/guide-for-men-who-are-serious-about-changing-part-2/ (For abusive men who are serious about changing.)

Hambrick, Brad. *Self-Centered Spouse: Help for Chronically Broken Marriages (Gospel for Real Life)* (Phillipsburg, NJ: P&R Publishing, 2014). (For caregivers)

Moles, Chris. *The Heart of Domestic Abuse: Gospel Solutions for Men Who Use Control and Violence in the Home* (Bemidji: MN: Focus Publishing, 2015). (For perpetrators or caregivers)

Domestic Violence Perpetrator Response Flowchart

The following flowchart is not intended to put process over people. We merely want to provide an at-a-glance guide that considers the safety of the victim as you determine whether or not to engage with a potential abuser.

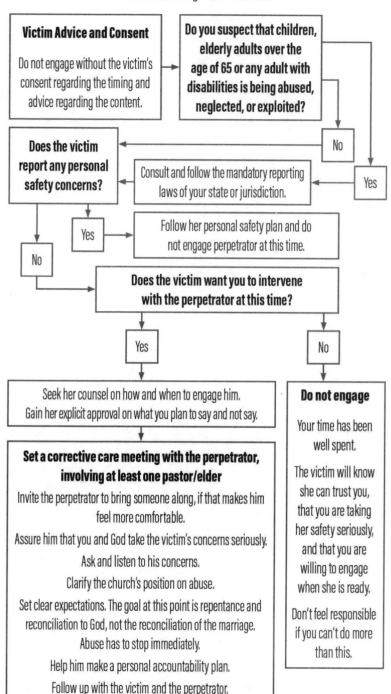

Victim Advice and Consent

Do not engage without the victim's consent regarding the timing and advice regarding the content.

Do you suspect that children, elderly adults over the age of 65 or any adult with disabilities is being abused, neglected, or exploited?

No

Yes

Does the victim report any personal safety concerns?

Consult and follow the mandatory reporting laws of your state or jurisdiction.

Yes

Follow her personal safety plan and do not engage perpetrator at this time.

No

Does the victim want you to intervene with the perpetrator at this time?

Yes

No

Seek her counsel on how and when to engage him. Gain her explicit approval on what you plan to say and not say.

Do not engage

Your time has been well spent.

The victim will know she can trust you, that you are taking her safety seriously, and that you are willing to engage when she is ready.

Don't feel responsible if you can't do more than this.

Set a corrective care meeting with the perpetrator, involving at least one pastor/elder

Invite the perpetrator to bring someone along, if that makes him feel more comfortable.

Assure him that you and God take the victim's concerns seriously.

Ask and listen to his concerns.

Clarify the church's position on abuse.

Set clear expectations. The goal at this point is repentance and reconciliation to God, not the reconciliation of the marriage. Abuse has to stop immediately.

Help him make a personal accountability plan.

Follow up with the victim and the perpetrator.

6

Considering Collateral Damage

Trauma is not what happens to us, but what we hold inside in the absence of an empathetic witness.—Gabor Maté[1]

My friends and companions stand aloof from my plague,
  and my nearest kin stand far off. (Ps. 38:11)

In bomb strikes, the closer an object is to the target, the greater the destruction. Domestic abuse is a relational bomb strike, and the damage does not stay contained to the intended target. Those most affected are *in* the home. Children, grandparents, and other extended family who may live in the home are all susceptible to the collateral damage. But those *around* the

---

1. Gabor Maté, Forward. In Peter Levine, *In an Unspoken Voice: How the Body Releases Trauma and Restores Goodness* (Berkeley, CA: North Atlantic Books, 2010), xii.

home suffer also—extended family who don't live in the home, friends of the family, and neighbors. Parents, in-laws, siblings, and friends often take on the role of caregivers in the fallout of domestic violence. Perhaps some of you reading this book now are nearer to ground zero than you ever imagined, and the discovery of what has been going on behind closed doors has been disorienting and painful. Even the family's church community may be breathing the toxic air polluted by the detonation. In this chapter, we want to help you consider the secondary trauma incurred by those in and around the family when home hurts.

Those who have experienced the collateral damage of domestic abuse wrestle with everything from disbelief and confusion, to anger and vengeance; from guilt and shame to disillusionment and depression. Family members often form sides and rally people to theirs. Often victims of abuse think disclosure isn't worth all the family tumult. Our hope in this chapter is to provide principles for wise care for the family system, recognizing that you, the reader, may be a part of that system. If that's you, we hope that you will learn some principles that will help you care for yourself as well.

Because it's a common question we get, we'll start by discussing reporting. As stated earlier, there is generally no legal obligation to report abuse of adults, unless the victim is elderly or disabled. And we also said that reporting in such cases can often pose additional threats to the victim. However, we also have stated that it is morally and usually legally imperative to report any suspicion of abuse or neglect of vulnerable parties such as children, the elderly, and the disabled.[2] Though state

---

2. We hope that chapter 4 made clear that asking the spouse being victimized by abuse if any children or other vulnerable parties, such as the elderly or disabled, in the home have also been harmed, or are in danger of being harmed, is a vital part of intervention. You are certainly ethically, and in most cases legally, responsible to report to

laws vary regarding mandating reporting, the ethical principle of protecting the weak and vulnerable among us is clear in Scripture (Matt. 18:6; 25:31-46). **We strongly urge you to know and observe the mandatory reporting laws in your state.**

As we care for those primarily impacted by domestic abuse, the victim and the abuser, we don't want to forget to care for those secondarily impacted. We'll start with remembering those in the home, the children and other vulnerable parties, before remembering those *around* the home—the larger family and others impacted.

Remember the Children (and Other Vulnerable Parties) in the Home

Children, the disabled, and elderly in a home that hurts can be impacted by domestic abuse in three ways. They can witness the abuse *indirectly*, such as by overhearing it from their room. Almost everyone who is in a home that hurts is at least an indirect witness to the abuse, as it is practically impossible to live in an abusive environment and not experience it, at least indirectly. Many of these people in the home are actually experiencing the abuse *directly*. While many parents who are living with an abusive partner believe that their children are generally unaware of the abuse, the children themselves tell a much different story. When asked, roughly 90 percent claimed that they had directly witnessed the violence.[3] Unfortunately,

---

authorities immediately if you become aware of, or in some cases even suspect, violence against children, the elderly, or the disabled. You are responsible for knowing and following what your state laws mandate regarding abuse reporting in your state. We hope that the resources in Appendix C will be helpful to you in this regard.

3. 'When Children Witness Violence,' domesticshelters.org, November 5, 2014 accessed January 26, 2021, https://www.domesticshelters.org/articles/childhood-domestic-violence/when-children-witness-violence

in addition to witnessing abuse indirectly or directly, some children and other vulnerable parties in a home that hurts are actually hurt themselves—*abused or neglected* by those whom God has placed in their lives to protect them. Children exposed to domestic violence, even indirectly, are much more likely to actually be abused themselves—as much as fifteen times more likely.[4] We contend that all of those living in a home that hurts witness the abuse at least indirectly. But many also witness it directly—and even experience it personally.

Remember, abuse is as much about perception as behavior. An abuser sees the world through the lenses of his desires and relates to others accordingly, positioning them to get what he wants. That corrupted way of seeing rubs off on the children and others in the home. Children raised witnessing abuse of a parent are lied to about the nature of human relationships, of gender roles, of authority, and especially of the character of God the Father. This often results in significant dysfunction later in childhood, adolescence, and adulthood.[5] As we have said, and will say again later, one of the comorbidities that is often associated with abusers is childhood trauma. It is not unusual that the abuser was himself abused as a child.

Thankfully, these effects are not inalterable. Christians who surround the family can model the good design of God in their

---

4. Blake Griffin Edwards, 'Alarming Effects of Children's Exposure to Domestic Violence,' Psychology Today, February 26, 2019, accessed January 26, 2021, https://www.psychologytoday.com/us/blog/progress-notes/201902/alarming-effects-childrens-exposure-domestic-violence.

5. Brett V. Brown and Sharon Bzostek, 'Violence in the Lives of Children,' *Crosscurrents*, 1. Bethesda, MD: Child Trends, 2003. Accessed January 26, 2021. http://www.childtrends.org/wp-content/uploads/2003/01/2003-15ViolenceChildren.pdf

    Lundy Bancroft and Jay G. Silverman, 'Assessing Risk to Children from Batterers,' in Peter G. Jaffe, Linda L. Baker, and Alison J. Cunningham, *Protecting Children from Domestic Violence: Strategies for Community Intervention* (New York: Guilford Press, 2004).

relationships; this can do a world of good to a child whose home life is full of lies. Caregivers can provide an empathetic witness by embodying love, grace, and truth.

Children who witness abuse are often sad, angry, or scared without fully understanding why. You can tell them why: They are upset for a good reason, since God made husbands to love their wives, not to harm them.

Children who witness abuse are receiving false messages about how a family relates to one another, what marriage is like, how men should treat women, and a whole host of other ways of seeing the world. All of this has to do with God. As with the victim herself, abuse warps the perception of children who witness it, including their understanding and their emotional responses.

The moral compass that Scripture calls *the conscience* is in the heart of every child. But living in an abusive home pulls that needle in every direction but north. Living under such a discrepancy between what their conscience says is right and what they see displayed causes a tension they can't explain. They can't put words to the emotional turmoil of watching someone they love harmed by someone else that they love, of not being able to predict when it will happen, of not being able to stop it when it does. This is traumatic, and may require counseling with someone skilled in working with traumatized children.

In the short term, you are simply affirming their feelings from Scripture. Specifically, you acknowledge that what they've witnessed is wrong, and they are correct to feel it as wrong. Abuse is the opposite of what God intended for marriage. God made a husband to love his wife, never to harm her. Use Scripture to affirm that their feelings are showing how God feels about the situation. (The Psalms are filled with examples, including 10:17-18; 27:10-14; 56:1-13.)

Children who witness abuse will be concerned about the safety of their abused parent. You should affirm your love and ongoing care not only for the children, but also for the abused parent.

Remember that kids in this situation live under the distress of seeing someone they love constantly threatened. They likely have tried to protect their abused parent in various ways, both directly in the moment and indirectly by trying to prevent the moment. Or, they may feel guilty for being too scared to try. Being unable to stop the pain of their parent is its own burden, which children will feel to varying degrees depending on age and personality.

Regardless, you should affirm your love for their hurting parent and your dedication to their good. Tell them that this is what God has called you to in loving their family. You are simply obeying Jesus, who loves their family more than you ever could (1 John 3:18).

Children who witness abuse may also be concerned for the abuser. You should affirm your love for the abuser, even as you work against his abuse.

Children are designed by God to love their parents, and this instinct is wonderfully generous and without condition. You must be mindful of this when talking about the abusive parent. A child can be simultaneously scared of, angry at, and enamored with his parent. He can understand that what he's seeing is not good while also not being confident in his own ability to make that call. You have to make that call for the child, but with words that convey love nevertheless. As a church leader, you should be able to speak about sin with a strong voice and soft eyes.

Explain to them that when you love someone, sometimes you have to stop them. You don't do this to be mean, but for their own good. You can illustrate this in a number of ways.

Here's one: Have you ever seen a bully on the playground? He wants other kids to do what he wants, so sometimes he scares them, sometimes he threatens them, and sometimes he hits them. Let me ask you a question: Who should stop that bully? Should it be the parents of the kids getting hurt or the parents of the bully himself? The parents of the bully should stop him because they love him and don't want him to be an evil person.

You cannot make any promises to the children about what will happen to their parents. But you can assure them that you will do your best to care for everyone in the way God says is best, whatever happens. And more importantly, you can assure them that the Lord cares deeply about what is happening in their lives, and will show them special grace to trust Him. Use familiar word pictures, like a shepherd caring for sheep (Ps. 23), a light in darkness (Ps. 18:28), or a hiding place in a storm (Ps. 32:7).

Remember the Larger Family and Others Around the Home

As a church leader, you will have varying degrees of responsibility for the larger family. In many situations, you will have no oversight (or even access) to the extended family, and thus no direct responsibility for them. But in many other situations, the larger family will be part of your church. The challenge here is not to over-involve them in the process (especially in the early stages where prudence is vital for safety to the victim) but also not to ignore their vital role for caring for the victim, holding the abuser accountable, and contributing to peace at church.

Families will respond in different ways, but will commonly have a specific set of harmful responses. What you should perhaps be most aware of in ministering to the larger family is that they will potentially be weighed down by a number of different responses that hinder progress in this situation.

Families will have different levels of awareness of the situation.
Unless the abused spouse has asked you to help them disclose the situation to the family, you should not be a source of information to them. It's too easy to cause more havoc through partial information being given to the wrong person at the wrong point in time. Your role is more focused on helping them to process biblically the information they've already received.

Some members of the family will just be discovering what's been going on, while others will have suspected it for a while. Some will be resistant to believing things are that bad, while others will be thrown into panic. Our advice is not to assume anything about either their level of knowledge nor how they're processing what knowledge they do have. When it comes to information, you should see yourself as an observer, not a source.

If you are asked for more details, you can simply tell them you are doing your best to serve everyone in the situation the best you can—and that means being extra careful with your words. Usually such an appeal resonates with people, even if they're unhappy with not knowing certain details. You model for them stability and trustworthiness, even if they don't immediately recognize it as such.

Families will have different perspectives of abuse generally.
Some family members will be unfamiliar with the dynamics of abuse, and thus not know how serious it is. Others will be actively hostile to the idea that abuse is a big deal, dismissing the concern as someone's social agenda. Still others will be so alarmed by the idea of abuse that they lose a reasonable perspective, reacting in a way that only makes life harder for

the victim. Again, you are largely observing how they respond so that you can bring biblical clarity to the situation.

Part of your ministry to the family can be instruction. We hope the framework we laid out in the first three chapters of this book is a helpful way of describing abuse biblically, and we encourage you to use it in helping the family understand. The most common question we receive from family members about the idea of abuse is *What actually constitutes abuse?* Remember the particular demarcation of abuse we laid out: A person acts abusively when he uses his personal strength to limit the strength of someone under his influence so they can be controlled. *Me over you* instead of merely *me before you.*

Families may need help fortifying their convictions about abuse. Only a fortified conviction will lead to decisive action. Your conviction should model for them God's hatred of abuse because it violates His character—a hatred that drives Him to stand boldly against it (Ps. 146:1-10; Prov. 14:31; Luke 17:1-4).

Families will have different perspectives of the couple specifically.
Beyond their opinion of abuse as an idea, family members will have opinions about the couple specifically. Remember, the term 'victim' does not capture a person entirely—that victim is also a sister, daughter, niece, and/or cousin who is known in the family as pleasant or annoying, respectable or gossipy, or any number of opinions family members have about one another. If family members are inclined toward her relationally, they are more prone to believe her and to respond resolutely. If they are inclined against her relationally, they will be more skeptical and less decisive in their actions.

To make matters more complicated, the abusive spouse often has a better reputation in the family, since he may be more conscious about cultivating the image of a stable home. It may be hard for family members to believe he is capable of the cruelty he's being accused of. It feels unloving to be willing to believe that about a family member, especially such a great guy. This is where you'll need to guide their thinking with a hardy understanding of sin—specifically, that sin is not just individual actions, but subtle patterns that shape the way a person relates to others, especially in private (see Rom. 1:28-32).

The family of an abuse victim often experiences extreme anger at the abuser, leading them to respond in harmful ways.

Anger can be an appropriate response to abuse, but has great potential to move to something inappropriate. Anger is related to a person's concept of what is right or wrong. Anger is in part a moral judgment about the situations and people that surround us (James 1:19-20). Anger at abuse can be an accurate moral judgment. How do we know this? Because God is angry at abuse. Injustice has been done. A person with greater power or influence has used it to harm someone with less.

But anger can also be inappropriately channelled. A family member's experience of anger is inadequate to accomplish anything. Only God's anger can bring about real judgment. A person's anger usually tries to accomplish something less, like vengeance. Family members will often be provoked by their anger to have hostile contact with the abuser—from text threats and social media shaming to destruction of an abuser's property or even physical assault. Most often, anger can plunge a family member into dark fantasies of revenge. You may even find Christian people fearful of the anger that has captured their minds.

To minister well to angry families, it will be helpful to keep a few things in mind. First, show them that God resonates with their anger, but He alone is the judge. Romans 12:17-21 speaks of God's wrath as a real, living force that is far more effective than any human anger. Second, show them that God does more than resonate with their anger, but acts on it. He will condemn the abuser for this, or if the abuser cries out to God in true repentance, He will place the condemnation on the cross of Christ. Those are the only two options God gives Himself. Either way, justice will be done in God's timing and in God's way. What God chooses is best.

The family of an abuse victim often experiences disillusionment at their own lack of control, leading them to respond in harmful ways.

The revelation of abuse will reveal to the family their own inability to protect even one they love so much. The word *disillusionment* is appropriate here because a family is dispelled of an illusion so precious to middle class Westerners: that we can keep the ones we love safe through careful vigilance. It's painful to have this illusion broken, and many family members—perhaps dads and brothers especially—will be hurting.

This can lead to any number of harmful responses. One can be the attempt to regain the control they presumed they had in the first place. They may try to put the lock-down on their loved one who has suffered abuse in an effort to protect her. They may take on an 'I told you so, and now I have to take charge' attitude, even if they would never say these words. Sometimes the one who suffered abuse prefers this, as she may have lost confidence in her own ability to manage her life. But this does not move her to greater responsibility and faithfulness.

Another harmful response that's more understandable, yet also unhelpful is seeking to get to the bottom of the *why* question. Knowledge can be an attempt at control, and trying to understand *the cause of this particular abuse* can lead to speculation that pulls a lot of energy away from moving forward in faith. The *why* question can drive family members apart rather than together. Specifically, it can drive them to blame—

an attempt to assign fault for anything related to the abuse. It can also drive them to over-explain—a constant re-describing of the factors that led to the abuse. These descriptions may be accurate, but they do not necessarily lead someone forward. But families can get stuck in this cycle.

To minister well to disillusioned families, you will need to remind them that God Himself describes this world as dangerous, and no one can escape the threat of living under the sun (Eccles. 4:1-3). At least, for now. Scripture keeps us grounded in the hard reality of life in a world not yet redeemed. But Scripture does more than acknowledge the grit of where we are; it expands our vision to include something greater. You will also need to remind disillusioned families that God answers our *why* questions not with explanations of His specific purposes, but with descriptions of Himself. 'When you pass through the waters, *I* will be with you; and through the rivers, they shall not overwhelm you; when you walk through fire you shall not be burned, and the flame shall not consume you. For *I am the Lord your God, the Holy One of Israel, your Savior*' (Isa. 43:2-3a, emphasis ours).

The family of an abuse victim often experiences guilt for failing to perceive, believe, or predict what was going on behind closed doors, leading them to respond in harmful ways.

As we said in the last point, disillusionment is painful. An added layer of pain is guilt, and guilt is complex. It's complex because, like so many of our experiences, it can have an element of accuracy and of inaccuracy. Family members may have actually sinned against their loved one by ignoring requests for help for any number of reasons, perhaps the most common being either a lazy resistance to getting involved or a judgmental, dismissive spirit. If family members feel guilt for ways they sinned, the solution is not to wallow in the guilt, but to repent and seek forgiveness (Matt. 5:23-24).

But often the guilt is inaccurate. Feeling guilty for not knowing abuse was occurring has some false assumption behind it—namely, that human beings are capable of knowing what is not revealed to them. A family member condemning himself because 'I should have been able to figure it out' or 'I should have trusted my gut' assumes that people can know information they don't have access to. The tragedy of abuse is that an abuser actively deceives others. The deceit is the fault of the deceiver, not the ones deceived.

As you minister to family members feeling such false guilt, encourage them to embrace their limitations as something God has given. They are not omniscient, like God. In fact, God made the difference between His limitless knowledge and their limited knowledge as one of the primary ways we know Him as Creator and ourselves as creatures (Acts 17:24-27). Family members need to face the hard truth that they *couldn't* have known, *couldn't* have predicted, and *couldn't* have stopped it. Trusting God means believing that the limitations He designed us with are good and wise. As humans, we wish we had more powers than we've been given and assume we would bring about a better world if we did. But we would not.

The family of an abuse victim often experiences apprehension about how to discuss what happened with their hurting loved one, leading to unhelpful interactions.

One thing you learn for certain over years of counseling: People are not good at putting words to their ideas. They are not even good at knowing what their ideas are in the first place. This is especially true in distressing situations. Families will need help understanding their own responses and communicating those responses to one another. In other words, they'll need help having good conversations.

It's all too easy for hurting family members to be reactive in the way they talk to one another. Two of the more common harmful ways of interacting are, on one hand, being dismissive and, on the other, being indulgent. Being dismissive is basically being unwilling to seek to understand the pain of the victim. Family members can speak to their abused loved one as if her experience does not need to be worked through. The attitude can be too matter-of-fact: The abuse happened, and now it's time to move on. Talking about it seems like an unnecessary hindrance to moving on.

Being indulgent, on the other hand, means simply talking through the pain without ever compelling the victim beyond their pain to something better. This occurs when family members only sympathize and never offer an encouraging word. Abuse becomes the center of every conversation, reinforcing an over-identification with their status as victim. This hinders the person from seeing themselves from a broader, more faith-filled perspective. It's a delicate but necessary tension between sympathizing with a victim's suffering and challenging them to responsible action that moves them beyond it.

Jesus maintained this tension in His approach to people. He is able to speak with infinite compassion for our suffering even as He compels us to take action in response to it. We have no record of Jesus speaking directly to a victim of domestic violence, but we have plenty of examples of Him speaking with victims of terror, oppression, and abuse at the hands of people more powerful than they were. One particularly instructive passage conveys His words to the suffering church of Smyrna. He says both 'I know your tribulation and your poverty' and 'Be faithful unto death' (Rev. 2:8-11). Sympathy for pain *and* encouragement to action. Family members will need help having conversations that keep this healthy tension.

Closing

Domestic violence causes all kinds of havoc in all kinds of lives. You won't possibly be able to mitigate all of the collateral damage it does. But we hope this chapter provided some insight into it, so that you can minister wisely to a variety of people caught up in a tragic situation.

Section 3

How to Care in the Long Term

The previous section was intended to help you through the process of caring for a victim in the wake of a disclosure of abuse and, eventually, confronting her abuser. This section you are about to read is intended to help you think through longer-term care considerations for both victim and abuser. In addition, we want to help church leaders know how to address abuse publicly in the congregation.

In a book of this length, we are not trying to provide comprehensive care strategies. We hope to offer biblical guidelines for ongoing care that utilize whatever resources are available to the parties involved.

The three chapters that make up this section will guide you to care well for everyone involved, including the church community.

7

From Victim to Overcomer

When someone lives with an abusive, destructive, manipulative and/or deceitful person, it definitely takes its toll on his or her mental, emotional, physical, and spiritual health. Being sane from God's perspective involves knowing, believing, and walking in the truth.—Leslie Vernick[1]

Fear not, for I am with you;
  be not dismayed, for I am your God;
I will strengthen you, I will help you,
  I will uphold you with my righteous right hand.
(Isa. 41:10)

---

1. Leslie Vernick, *The Emotionally Destructive Marriage: How to Find Your Voice and Reclaim Hope* (Colorado Springs, CO: WaterBrook, 2013), 70.

In Chapter 4, we addressed how to care for the victim in the aftermath of a disclosure of abuse and how to help her and any child victims gain some level of personal safety. Hopefully, she is now taking steps toward safety, and feels supported by you and her community in taking the steps that she needs to take toward healing. She needs your support now more than ever. It is important to insure that those caring for her in the church are in this for the long haul. In this chapter, we will discuss the longer-term strategy to help a victim process what happened to her and begin to heal.

We want to encourage you at the outset not to assume safety (physical, sexual, emotional, financial, digital, or spiritual) just because we are now talking about longer-term considerations. She may be paying dearly for the courageous action she took in disclosing the abuse and standing up to her abuser. Whether the couple remains under the same roof, is separated, or is even moving toward divorce,[2] the abuse is likely still continuing. **Proximity is not necessary for abuse to continue, although proximity does generally increase the risk of imminent danger.** He could be threatening her, stalking her, removing financial support, using the children to get to her, minimizing, denying, blaming, or any number of other abusive behaviors, regardless of physical proximity. Whether she has chosen to separate or to stay, she may well need a revised personal safety plan, because there are potential dangers either way. If she is separated from her abuser, which is common and often even recommended for safety and a better chance at healing, she still requires all the elements of ongoing support that we mentioned in Chapter 4. In addition, she may require some support with finding housing, finances, child care, transportation, and other

---

2. See Appendix B: FAQs on Separation, Divorce, and Reunification after Abuse for help on these difficult topics.

practical forms of support. If there are any safety concerns, she may need to consider a protective order.

She may have chosen to stay in the home, perhaps on the basis of some of the logistical concerns named above. If so, her personal safety plan should include ways of keeping herself and any children (or other vulnerable parties) safe in their own residence, as well as getting herself and other vulnerable parties to safety in the event that he escalates. We would encourage her to maintain a 'go bag' for herself and for all other vulnerable parties, in case there is a need for a quick departure.

Whether she stays or goes, she will need ongoing pastoral care and it will be important that you set realistic expectations on standards of care, to guard against unrealistic expectations. And whether she stays or goes, she ideally should be receiving trauma counseling from an experienced counselor trained in trauma counseling *and* have an experienced and trained advocate caring for her.[3]

If we were to use common vernacular, this chapter is about caring for a victim as she moves from *victim* to *survivor*.[4] These terms can be helpful, but only as circumstantial identifiers, not core identities. This distinction is vital to grasp. *Victim* and *survivor* are merely descriptions of a person in relation to the abuse that has occurred to her. They do not capture the core identity of a person. The person you are ministering to is

---

3.   In your locality, it may not be possible to have both a counselor and an advocate for the victim, and both a counselor and a shepherding/accountability team for the abuser, but we consider it ideal to have bigger teams involved in domestic abuse cases where possible.

4.   See Chapter 2 as a refresher on how we use this terminology. Specifically, we have been using the term *victim* to refer to the person who has been abused or is currently being abused. We are using the term *survivor* to refer to the person who once was a victim of abuse and is now safe from the more oppressive effects of the abuse, though still dealing with its ongoing implications.

primarily an image-bearer of God and, if redeemed by Christ, a beloved child of God.

So at this point of transition, let's remind ourselves of the overall goal. You are helping a person who is designed to reflect the personhood of God to respond in faith to the abuse that occurred to her. This includes seeing herself in the way God sees her, and not in the way she's been conditioned by abuse to see herself. As you help her grow into the fullness of this identity, you are also helping her relate differently to the abuse that has occurred to her. That's what we mean when we say that you're helping move her from *victim* to *survivor*. But a term that may better capture how a person's faith can grow in how she relates to her past abuse is *overcomer*.

The apostle John uses *overcomer* to describe how a Christian relates to the enemies of the soul, the forces that press against a Christian's ability to see God clearly and to continue trusting in His love (1 John 5:4-5). Abuse is part of the evil work of a darkened world, and a Christian is sustained by God to overcome the deeds of darkness and have victory over them.

But victory in this life is a partial, often delicate, victory. It is an ongoing set of victories, rather than one big conclusive one. That one doesn't come until Jesus makes all things new.

Ongoing Victories

If a victim is no longer being victimized, if bruises have healed or she no longer breathes air full of harsh words, what is the goal of ongoing care? Well, first, as we have stated above, bringing the abuse to light often makes it worse, not better. Safety and freedom from abuse cannot be assumed simply because the abuse is in the light. Until her abuser is able to successfully complete the work that we will be discussing in Chapter 8, and has truly demonstrated godly sorrow with new, non-abusive behavior walked out over a significant period of time, he must still be regarded as abusive, or at least potentially abusive. Even if bruises have healed and harsh words have subsided, he may pivot to more covert and subversive forms of abuse. This is something that both the victim and those caring for her should be alert to.

Secondly, her body and her soul are still suffering from the very real effects of her abuse. If you've ever gone backpacking with sixty or more pounds, you've experienced opposition, particularly if you were hiking uphill. The longer you toil under this weight, the more adjustments your body makes to the weight of the pack, the angle of the climb, the points on your body where the straps dig in. When you take the backpack off to simply walk on level ground, you look and feel like a crazy person, leaning forward and taking each step with the same mechanical thrusts. You can't right yourself, even though you are no longer under the burden that opposed you for so long. Why? Your body had adjusted to the opposition in order to survive the hike.

Often victims of abuse only realize the effect it had on them after they are out of immediate danger. It's not until the opposition is removed that they realize they are still reeling.

The present chapter is intended to help you understand these long-term concerns, which may feel much less urgent than her initial safety, but are no less important. The initial disclosure and safety plan started the journey, and she should continue with that safety plan and with your steadfast support as she works toward healing. Her path to healing will take some ongoing travel. Her abuser is still somewhere on his own path of seeing, owning, hating, and turning (or not) from his sin, while at the same time working through his own corrupt perception and behavior—things like entitlement, objectification, control, false beliefs about God, self, and others, hiding his shadow self from himself and others, shame, his own past traumas, etc. We'll discuss his process in the next chapter. For now, recognize that her healing may be blocked often, if not constantly, by his further abuse. Thus her journey of knowing, believing, and walking in the truth often occurs in a constant context of residual abuse or reminders of abuse. Since the contours of each person's experience are different, we cannot provide a topographical map for every journey. But we can provide a plan to read these features for yourself.

We will help you read both the condition of your traveler and some of the milestones of progress on the journey out. Specifically, we'll first provide a framework to help you consider how abuse has affected the person by explaining the concept of trauma. Then, with that awareness of how trauma may be shaping her present responses, we will suggest ways to help redeem her understanding of self, her relationships with others, and, most importantly, her intimacy with God.

Trauma and Personal Response

It's easy for someone victimized by abuse to feel misunderstood by others, especially by anyone who has a degree of authority in her life. You may even get the sense that she's preloaded to feel judged or dismissed by anything you say. If you consider what she's been through, you shouldn't be surprised. She probably feels like she herself doesn't understand what she's going through, and naturally doubts if anyone else does. She is not wrong to have these doubts. Even well-meaning people who want to encourage her can do so without considering how she will receive it, given the state of her heart.

This is why thinking carefully about trauma is important. To enter into a helping relationship with a victim of abuse without at least a basic understanding of the traumatic damage done is like trying to administer first-aid to someone with internal injuries that aren't obvious. You could actually do far more damage to the person because of the significant injuries that aren't readily apparent. We want to give you eyes for trauma as you care for victims so that you don't cause further harm. We introduced the concept of trauma as the damage done by abuse in Chapter 2. We discussed secondary trauma and the collateral damage of abuse in Chapter 6. We will now more fully address the victim's trauma, as well as an overview of her process of healing in this chapter.

Trauma Described

Like all complex concepts, trauma can be described in a number of different ways. Our goal is to describe trauma consistent with the way that we introduced it theologically in Chapter 2. There, we attempted to describe abuse as a desecration of God's design for people to relate to one another in love. While love builds others up, abuse tears them down. Abuse breaks down and limits the personal capacity of others so they are easier to control. The overwhelming effect of these forced limits on the personal capacities of abuse victims, both seen and unseen, is trauma.[5]

Trauma is the limiting effect on a victim from her abuser's repeated attempts to control her. Her capacities as a divine image bearer are diminished—specifically, her capacity to think, to desire, and to make choices for herself in a way free from the intrusion of the consequences she lives under. This

---

5. Peter A. Levine says 'we become traumatized when our ability to respond to a *perceived* threat is in some way overwhelmed.' Levine goes on to add, 'In short, trauma is about loss of connection—to ourselves, to our bodies, to our families, to others, and to the world around us.' (*Healing Trauma: A Pioneering Program for Restoring the Wisdom of Your Body* [Boulder, CO: Sounds True, 2008], 9.)

hinders how she responds to life—both how she sees her life and how she acts in it.

Even after a victim is safe from any immediate threat from her abuser, how she responds to life will be constrained to some degree by what happened to her. Specifically, trauma is the effect on how she responds to other people, how she sees herself, and most importantly, how she sees God.

Not all victims are affected by trauma in the same way or to the same degree.[6] But generally speaking, the more extreme or longstanding the abuse, the more devastating the trauma. The more devastating the trauma, the more gradual the process of restoration. Trauma is stored in the victim's body and in her soul. This makes sense, according to God's design of people as embodied souls.

As we mentioned in Chapter 2, victims carry trauma in their physical bodies in a variety of ways. Trauma survivors may experience panic attacks, fatigue, disturbances of sleep or appetite, chronic pain in various parts of the body, tension in various parts of the body, digestive issues, and a variety of other seemingly 'unexplainable' physical issues. In fact, sometimes the appearance of these physical symptoms, which doctors are not able to attribute to a medical diagnosis, act as an alarm system, awakening the victim to the abuse that she is experiencing.

Trauma also crushes the soul of a person. You can think of an abused person as a person who has been living in a world of lies, powerfully reinforced with its own internal 'justice' system,

---

6. 'No matter how frightening an event may seem, not everyone who experiences it will be traumatized.' Peter A. Levine with Ann Frederick, *Waking the Tiger: Healing Trauma* (Berkeley, CA: North Atlantic Books, 1997), 28. This is very important when coming alongside trauma victims in the church. You should never assume that trauma hasn't occurred just because you or others would not find a particular event or pattern of events traumatic. Every individual's traumatic threshold is different, as is everyone's experience of trauma. Never discount or dismiss another person's experience of trauma.

which she gradually internalized so she could survive. Even when she removes herself from the abuse, she will carry those false ideas with her. She may struggle to regulate her emotions. She may appear to always be on high alert, her head always 'on a swivel.' This is called hypervigilance, and is quite common for trauma survivors. She may have problems concentrating or remembering things. (And these particular symptoms of trauma will often be used against her by her abuser and his allies, who may accuse her of lying when her accounts of the abuse don't seem consistent.) She will often relate to others differently, guarding herself in certain ways because of the unrecognized value for self-protection that's now more central to her motivations.[7]

Other soul-crushing effects can include depression, for a number of possible reasons, including a sense of failure or a false guilt for 'betraying' her husband. She will likely be constantly anxious, stressed, and overwhelmed. She may have trouble making even basic decisions after living for years with someone who stole that right from her.[8] Relationally, she may avoid thoughts, feelings, places, activities, people and/or conversations that bring up painful associations for her. The residual shame of staying in or having to flee a destructive marriage may contribute to the distance she feels from other Christians, as she compares what she knows about her life situation to what she doesn't know about the life situations of

---

7. '...traumatized people have a tendency to superimpose their trauma on everything around them and have trouble deciphering whatever is going on around them.' Bessel van der Kolk, *The Body Keeps The Score: Brain, Mind, and Body in the Healing of Trauma* (New York: Penguin Books, 2014), 17. We highly recommend Dr. van der Kolk's insightful work in understanding how emotional trauma is stored in the body.

8. 'Trauma results in a fundamental reorganization of the way mind and brain manage perceptions. It changes not only how we think and what we think about, but also our very capacity to think.' Bessel van der Kolk, 21.

others. Or, she may struggle with doubts about the Lord—His goodness, His wisdom, His nearness, His justice, or His love.

Our goal in discussing trauma in this section is not to make you a trauma expert, but rather to make you aware of its very real effect on the person you're helping. If you are in a role of providing care to a victim of abuse, please take time to educate yourself on trauma and the basics of trauma-informed care. If you do, you will find that the perception and behavior of the victim will make a lot more sense to you. We have included some excellent resources at the end of this chapter, and we reference others within the chapter.

Not Determinative, but Still Dominant

But traumatic effects are not the last word. As we said at the opening of the chapter, the person you are helping is not a victim in the sense that it is core to her identity. Rather, *in relation to the abuse that occurred to her* she is a victim. So here's a way to think about your care for her in this season: you are coming alongside her, in addition to a counselor with trauma experience, as she works to change the way she relates to the abuse that occurred to her. The corrupting effect that abuse had on her is not inalterable, though it is resistant. It is not determinative, though it is dominant.

How dominant trauma is in her perspective will vary by person and situation. Generally, the more severe and longstanding the abuse a person has endured, the more ascendant the traumatic effects on her perception of the world. Our hope is that the resource you're holding in your hands will increase your ability to ask into her experience and wisely help her to respond in new ways. But we also encourage the humility of recognizing the limits of your insights. You should encourage her to see (and help her find) a counselor who specializes in domestic abuse or trauma. The resources in Appendix C can help you find a counselor who specializes in trauma in your area. A specialist brings a level of insight into the particular complexities of the traumatic experience that the average church member, care advocate or pastor does not.[9] The greater the traumatic effects on a person, the more helpful such insights will be for helping them get to the point of thinking more clearly.

---

9. For example, the most common professional approach is based on Judith Herman's landmark work *Trauma and Recovery*, which is a three-phrase treatment model based on common effects of violence on people. This model is the current standard of care for complex trauma (the type of trauma that generally results from abuse) and has changed very little since its introduction in 1992. Judith Herman, *Trauma and Recovery: The Aftermath of Violence—From Domestic Abuse to Political Terror, 1R ed* (New York: Basic Books, 2015).

In brief, the goal of the first phase of treatment is safety and stabilization. This work was started during the initial response to victim care that we described in Chapter 4, when you encouraged the victim to develop a safety plan and begin meeting with a counselor trained in trauma. Many victims never progress beyond this phase of treatment, because safety and stability feels so good and the work required to process intense memories and emotions in phase two of treatment seems so daunting.

In the second phase of treatment, the story of the abuse is told and memories are processed and mourned. This phase is where specialization is perhaps most helpful, since experience teaches wisdom in *how to access and appropriately approach* a person based on what they can presently handle. The average church leader does not have the accumulated experience to make these judgment calls in more severe situations.

In the third phase of treatment, the goal is to move beyond the past to develop a trauma-free identity. Specialists are aware of the common primary hindrances to a person seeing herself from a refreshed perspective, and that is where their training is most helpful. However, as we say in the main body of the text, this phase is where larger issues of life's meaning become more prominent, and thus pastoral guidance is more vital.

Ideally, each of us would have access to a counselor who is trained in, and has accumulated experience with, people traumatized by abuse. May such a tribe increase! But not all church leaders will have access to such resources. Our responsibility is to care for hurting people through the discerning use of the resources that are available.

We want to be clear that making use of a specialist as part of the church's ministry to a person victimized by abuse in no way undermines the sufficiency and authority of Scripture, nor does it undermine the responsibility of pastors to shepherd their people. Here's why: You are not handing the overall care of an individual over to professionals; rather, in your guidance of the person to see herself from God's perspective, you are utilizing the expertise professionals have about her traumatic experience. Her long-term spiritual care is the responsibility of her church.

Redeeming Personal Response

Now to get practical. Caring for someone victimized and traumatized by abuse over the long haul is multifaceted. It will take different types of ministries, different types of friendships, different types of resources, different types of skills and expertise. No one person could possibly provide all of these. Including you.

As a church leader or spiritual friend, your job is not to be everything this person needs. Rather, it is to help coordinate care toward a common goal. This section will begin by describing that central goal you will aim for, then describe practical components of long-term care that move her toward that goal.

The central goal of long-term care, from a spiritual perspective, is to be an 'empathetic witness'[10] who can, by

---

10. We love the use of this term in Gabor Maté's Foreword to Peter A. Levine, *In An Unspoken Voice: How the Body Releases Trauma and Restores Goodness* (Berkeley, CA: North Atlantic Books, 2010), xi-xii. From a Christ-centered perspective, an 'empathetic witness' is a witness to God's goodness and His redemption in the midst of incredibly dark and devastating circumstances. This witness is an empathetic one— one who seeks to understand and share in the victim's pain while pointing her to the Lord's redemptive purpose in her life.

God's grace, help a victim restore what the abuse destroyed in her perspective of herself, of relationships, and of the Lord most importantly. Faith in Jesus Christ is the power behind the process of restoring her ability to see her life rightly. Simply identifying lies she's believing and telling her truths to replace them is not sufficient. The lies were forced into her through relationship, and the truth must be modeled for her in relationship.

Specifically, you want to help her understand herself from God's perspective—that is, as a valued person able to express herself freely to the Lord and responsible before Him. If she belongs to Christ by faith, then she is also a beloved daughter. You also want to help her relate to others based on what God says about human relationships—that is, to be neither controlled by fear of them nor to return evil on them. Most importantly, you want to help her see God as He's revealed Himself—that is, as a heavenly Father who never forces obedience from His children, but compels them to obey by transforming their hearts. God is entirely trustworthy, never manipulative, stable in His judgment, and patient even when wronged. Whatever abuse is, God's love is the opposite.

As you work through her perspective of self, of others, and of the Lord, you will likely need to address a number of themes that bring clarity to each of these areas. These themes are truths from Scripture that counter some of the most egregious lies implicit in abuse.

Think of these lies not just as counterfeit facts, but as emotionally charged impressions. These lies are not just factually untrue, they carry with them a weight of value. Imagine, for instance, that a person's abuser repeatedly told her, 'You're worthless' while bursting out at her in anger when she expressed her own opinion. This lie is not only factually untrue, it also makes a lasting emotional impression because it carries with it passion and value. Abuse shrinks the perspective of a victim not just by pressing different ideas on her, but also by forcing conformity to different desires. An abuser wants her to value what *he* values—namely, his own comfort, honor, and will.

Your job as an empathetic witness caring for such a person is to seek understanding of the false impressions they now carry with them as part of how they see the world. You will need to listen well and ask good questions as you labor to understand. As you together come to see how these lies have affected her, you can then show how Scripture leaves an entirely different impression. Where abuse tells lies that leave a person diminished and fearful, God's Word gives truths that expand and enliven the soul. You embody those truths in a loving relationship that begins to undermine the impressions left by an abusive one.

What does it mean in practice for those caring for the abused to undermine false impressions with true ones? Such lies are undermined by first identifying what they are, and countering them with biblical truth. One person victimized by abuse will not necessarily struggle under the same set of lies as another. Abuse will have different effects on one person than on another, depending on a number of factors like personality and context. This puts a premium on listening carefully to *how* she tells her story. Whether she talks about her abuse a lot or a little, you are listening for clues into how she is perceiving herself, her relationship to other people, and her relationship to God.

You will likely see everything from anger and disillusionment to shame and guilt, from fear and anxiety to depression and despair. To guide you on what you may uncover, we want to lay out some common ideas victims of abuse form and the emotions and values attached to them. Remember, everyone is different, so not every victimized person will struggle with every one of these. It is important that you let her put her own words to her impressions. We offer the following insights not as phrases you impose on her, but as ideas you want to look out for.[11]

Impressions About Self

I'm not sure I can trust my own thoughts and emotions.
She will likely feel insecure about many of the decisions she has made as part of the process. She may even second guess the advice you've given her along the way as she begins to face the recent changes to her situation. She may feel uncertain that she's made the right decisions or even that she has the *ability* to make right decisions. She may feel like she doesn't know *what* to feel. Given what she may have been told what to think and feel for years, this shouldn't be surprising.

Acknowledge her insecurity as well as why she is likely experiencing it. Big decisions like this come with a lot of uncertainty, even under normal circumstances. Her confidence is not in how *certain* she is, but in God's promise to guide her through the means He has laid out in His Word: wise counselors, the community of saints, the guidance of the Spirit, and the truth of Scripture. If she is looking for a solid sense of certainty, she is looking for the wrong thing. Instead, she should be confident that God wants her to make choices for herself in dependent trust on Him. She can do it.

---

11. In addition to this section, you may find it helpful to review how we described in Chapter 3 the particular ways a victim's perceptions and behaviors are corrupted by the abuse they endure. See in particular the section entitled 'The Person Victimized by Abuse,' including subsections 'Perception Corrupted by Abuse' and 'Behavior Corrupted by Abuse.'

I'm ashamed for being part of such an awful marriage.
Shame is another likely part of her experience. It may seem obvious to you that a victim of abuse is not at fault for her abuse. But it's quite common for victims of abuse, who are often conditioned by their abusers to believe such lies. In her mind, she may think she could have shown him more respect, loved him more convincingly, or endured him with greater patience. Or, even if she knows the abuse was not her fault, she might feel shame for marrying him in the first place or not leaving sooner. Different people will feel shame for different reasons.

Acknowledge this shame and help her think biblically about it. Shame is the deeply engrained belief that her identity is determined by what she has done, what she has experienced, or what has been done to her. But her abuser doesn't get to determine her identity, her Creator does. She is an image-bearer of God. And if she is a believer, she is the beloved daughter of the King. She doesn't feel that right now, which is why she needs the people of God in her life to remind her of this truth.

I will always be damaged.
This is a form of hopelessness. In her mind, the pain and confusion she currently experiences will always be part of her experience. She's telling you that she is tired of fighting. And who could blame her? She has spent a significant portion of her life in an unhealthy and destructive relationship, leaving her feeling empty and defeated. Acknowledge the weariness she's experiencing and even the difficulty of envisioning anything better.

But Scripture is full of promises for this very situation. For instance, Joel 2:24-27 is a powerful testimony of God's delight in restoring what has been destroyed in the lives of His people, so that they shall 'eat in plenty and be satisfied, and praise the name of the Lord your God, who has dealt wondrously with you. And my people shall never again be put to shame' (v. 26). God's people will not always be damaged. Healing is possible. But it will take time.

Impressions About Other People

No one understands me.
This idea can be characterized by a mix of isolation, insecurity, even pride and shame. But regardless of the underlying characteristics, this is an idea about others that will be a hindrance to her growth.

Acknowledge that her experience is indeed unique to her. Scripture affirms that 'the heart knows its own bitterness, and no stranger shares its joy' (Prov. 14:10). This truth drives us to find our primary solace in the Lord. He alone can understand the sorrows that run deep within. But *understanding* can mean a few different things.

Someone can have sympathy—and wisdom—for a victim of abuse without having experienced abuse himself. God made us to be able to bear the burdens of others in ways that legitimately lighten their load (Gal. 6:2). For a victim to conclude that no one can understand her is to cut herself off from genuine help, and patient encouragement may be a vital part of helping her see others rightly.

I can't trust anyone, especially people in charge.
No one should be surprised that someone living under the unjust use of authority will be suspicious of authority in general. A victim learns to be painfully aware of the imbalances of power and influence that exist in human relationships. When she senses someone has a higher degree of either, she will likely feel more vulnerable and fearful in that person's presence. Church leaders—especially pastors, who hold a significant

degree of spiritual influence—must be aware of this difference, and adjust their approach accordingly.

Throughout this book, we've made suggestions to have as much advocacy available to the victim as possible. This is to care for her in her vulnerable state, but it is also to display to her a godly use of influence that builds her up, protects her, and allows her the freedom to follow the Lord from her own heart. This is the heart of those who are called to guard the people of God, as the apostle Paul makes clear. He could have made demands of His people, but He withheld that right, instead demonstrating a commitment to be 'gentle among you, like a nursing mother taking care of her own children' (1 Thess. 2:7). Trust is not something you teach in a lesson or assign as homework. It is something you establish through demonstrated selfless care over time.

Impressions About the Lord

God allowed me to live under such cruelty, so I cannot trust Him. Perhaps what is most important in helping a victim heal from the evil done to her is to restore her relationship to the source of all good. Suffering often lies to a person about God, causing them to doubt that He is good. When a victim wonders how a supposedly good God could allow such cruelty to happen to her, what she's wondering is a cosmic question people throughout time have wrestled with: What is God's relationship to the evil that occurred to me? It's a question you should not simply answer all at once, since wrestling is a process.

But here's a great place to start. You can give her full assurance of a truth that may never have occurred to her, especially if her abuser had intentionally misused Scripture to control her. Here it is: *The Lord hates what happened to you.*

Abuse is sin, and God hates sin more than anyone else is capable of hating something. It is contrary to His character and harmful to His good creation. It is a special kind of injustice that takes the good gifts God gave to men so that they could build others up, and turns it around for the opposite purpose, to tear others down. God hates the suffering of His people, and in fact voluntarily enters into their pain with a sympathy that cannot be described (Rom. 8:22-30). The goodness of God's character is the opposite of the cruelty she suffered, and is in fact the only thing that ultimately confirms the feeling inside her that abuse is wrong.

This will not solve the mystery of why God allows suffering. But that is not the burden of your ministry to her. The burden of your ministry is to assure her of God's heart, and give her hope that the evil she suffers is not a permanent burden. The Lord will personally wipe every tear she has ever cried from her face, which will one day shine like the sun in His presence (Rev. 21:4).

God is disappointed in me, so I can't go to Him for help.
The ongoing burden for some victims is the sheer disappointment of what they consider a ruined life. They even see their relationship with God through this lens of disappointment. What they expected from themselves and from life appears to have failed, and they figure this disappointment is just a reflection of God's attitude toward them. They may feel guilt from a variety of sins that were part of their response to the abuse occurring to them. It could be regarding the lengths she went to to hide the abuse, sinful pursuits she used to distract from the abuse, or even the inner hatred that seems so inescapable. Whatever she's feeling guilty for, she perceives God as disappointed in her.

But God does not experience disappointment like we do. When people don't meet our expectations, we harbor resentment, even if quietly so. But God knows both our weakness and our sinfulness, and His gracious disposition toward sinners remains. The one who acknowledges their own weakness receives the compassion of God: 'As a father shows compassion to his children, so the LORD shows compassion to those who fear him. For he knows our frame; he remembers that we are dust' (Ps. 103:13-14). The one who acknowledges her own sin will never be rejected, 'The sacrifices of God are a broken spirit; a broken and contrite heart, O God, you will not despise' (Ps. 51:17). Gently help her to see that her own disappointment with herself is not the best gauge of God's attitude toward her. What He says about Himself in His Word is.

God can save me from my sin, but I'm not so sure He can sort through this mess.
Christians often struggle to connect Scripture to their daily experience in normal situations. It's easy to acknowledge that God helps with our religious dilemmas—like forgiving our sins or guaranteeing our future salvation. It's much harder to acknowledge His present help in the messiness of our lives. This is particularly difficult in traumatic situations, where this connection is even harder to make, and the damage seems all the more catastrophic.

But you must encourage her not to underestimate the restorative power of God. For His children, He regularly turns their mourning into dancing, so that they might be dazzled by His goodness and sing His praises (Ps. 30:11-12). His plan of restoration is better than anything she may still be tempted to cling to. Part of caring for her is to help her see that she can trust what the Lord intends to restore, and release to Him what she envisions being restored. For instance, she may think that she'll never be happy unless the marriage is restored. This may or may not be part of God's providential will. So her future happiness cannot rise and fall with that particular point. Teach her to grieve the loss—or potential loss—of something God created good, but to trust that even if her marriage is not restored, her life certainly can be.

For all of these potential misgivings about the Lord and the myriad others that may arise, you love a victim well by listening to her, asking wise questions, and pointing her to the gracious, just, compassionate, and kindhearted Father who will prove Himself to be better than she's so far dared to imagine. Learning to trust God at His Word gradually builds true ideas, inspires more stabilizing emotions, and encourages self-controlled choices.

Components of Long-Term Care

Helping a person once victimized by abuse redeem her personal response will mean long-term care. But you cannot do this alone. No one person can. This is why the Church is essential to personal spiritual renewal. In all of its foibles and failures, God is redeeming His people as a community of faith.

The communal nature of our personal growth may at first seem particularly threatening to someone who has been abused. Given what we've described about how trauma warps perspective, this should not be surprising. But living among Christians who are learning to love as God loves is like entering a new atmosphere, far more oxygenated than the small, suffocating world of her abuser.

In this section, we will provide an overview of what long-term pastoral care can look like. This is not a care strategy per se, but rather an overview of the components that should be in place to help restore her to strength and joy in the Lord. We believe pastoral care long term should involve public, personal, and practice ministry.

Public Ministry of the Word

The public ministries of the Word are the regular church gatherings where the people of God join together under the Word of God. The powerful effect of singing, praying, and hearing Christ proclaimed should not be underestimated. Especially if a victim is attending these gatherings from a personal context of a newfound freedom, she will often experience them quite differently than she did while under constraint. Connecting her with the body of Christ is essential.

But *how* you connect her to these public gatherings will take some careful consideration in the form of both *public protection* and *public advocacy*. Every situation is different, but a few guiding principles for both of these may prove helpful.

A victim may need some form of public protection. The abuser may be hostile and actively threatening the victim, even if they are separated. Regarding public gatherings, help her be wise about her safety. It may be safest for her not to attend a public service, which is a predictable time and location. But if she decides she wants to, arranging special security measures for her can be a loving way to facilitate her participation with the congregation. If the abuser is not actively hostile, you still want to make any arrangement that facilitates the victim's unhindered participation in congregational life. This may be asking the abuser not to attend for a season, or if he does, requiring him to pair up with an assigned individual for accountability. But anyone who is shepherding or providing accountability to an abuser should be trained in the approach we are describing in this book. Otherwise, the abuser is likely to form an alliance with them and 'triangulate' them onto his 'side,' and against his victim. This is a common dynamic of abuser behavior that we will discuss more in the next chapter. You just need to be aware that this is common and likely.

A victim will also need public advocacy. Church size and service arrangement is different in every church, so it won't all look the same. But generally, people will know that something significant is happening in the home of this family. The pastors of the church demonstrate good leadership by helping the congregation be aware of the situation so that they can serve, but not told anything that should be kept private for the sake of the victim. Chapter 9 gives more guidance on leading the congregation through this.

Personal Ministry of the Word

Public ministries alone are not sufficient for long-term care. Healing comes through personal ministry of the Word as well, which may involve a number of components. The coordinating component is direct pastoral care, which coordinates other types of care, like specialized counseling, ministries and resources dedicated to abuse advocacy, and support relationships.

Pastoral care requires pastors and trained lay leaders who are willing to meet with a victim, listen to the latest developments in her situation and offer biblical guidance, as the previous section provided ideas for. Such meetings don't necessarily need to be weekly, but ought to have some regularity to them. Pastors and church leaders with more experience in victim care may find pastoral counseling effective by itself. But for those with less experience, making use of specialized counseling is wise. Often victims find their experience difficult to describe, and someone with experience can more effectively help them understand it. The ideal is experienced Christian counseling that approaches people from a biblical framework and is willing to coordinate with church leadership, with all the proper releases signed.

But at least equally important is the care of fellow church members. The Church builds itself up in love (Eph. 4:12), meaning that Christians form one another into maturity through being present enough in each others' lives to offer the kind of encouragement that counts. In many cases, this will happen naturally, with close friends in the church taking initiative. Other times, it may take some more planning by church leaders to ensure that a hurting person is surrounded with the right people. Whether the victim is highly connected or not, coordinating the care is a good idea. In our context, we have even had simple 'meet ups' on Sunday mornings or Wednesday nights for whoever is in a helping relationship to hear from each other in the hope of caring better for the victim.

Practical Care

In the same spirit, the people of God can rally around the one who is hurting with care for the countless practical needs that arise in these situations, both big and small. Someone coming out of abuse may need help with housing, banking, and legal matters. She may need help with communication with her spouse about the necessary matters of life, like the children or the upkeep of the house.

This is another shining example of how the church community can care far more extensively than the leadership could alone. With the victim's permission, you can recruit help from professionals in your congregation—lawyers, bankers, or real estate agents—as well as folks who have similar skill sets from related life experience. Those who lend a hand will find themselves encouraged by the privilege of serving and invested in the good outcome for the victim. This is another place where trained victim advocates can bless the church, the church staff, and the victim herself. Train members to be advocates for victims.[12]

The needs will change according to what develops in the situation, in the marriage, and in her own heart. Pastors, leaders, and members need to maintain awareness of those needs in order to help direct God's people to help.

Conclusion

Our intention in this chapter was to provide an overview of how to help someone move from victim to overcomer. Every life is different, so it's difficult to say how long care will last. Maybe the best thing to keep in mind is that the needs will change, and the main thing you can do is be aware of them so that you can provide appropriately.

Recommended Resources

Forrest, Joy. *Called to Peace Companion Workbook* (Raleigh, NC: Blue Ink Press, 2019).

Gingrich, Heather D. *Restoring the Shattered Self: A Christian Counselor's Guide to Complex Trauma* (Downers Grove, IL: InterVarsity Press, 2013).

Gingrich, Heather D. and Fred C. Gingrich. *Treating Trauma in Christian Counseling.* (Downers Grove, IL: InterVarsity Press, 2017).

---

12. See the resource list in Appendix C for victim advocate training options.

Herman, Judith. *Trauma and Recovery: The Aftermath of Violence—From Domestic Violence to Political Terror.* (New York: Basic Books, 1992).

Holcomb, Justin S. and Lindsey A. Holcomb. *Is It My Fault: Hope and Healing for Those Suffering Domestic Violence.* (Chicago, IL: Moody Publishers, 2014).

Tracy, Celestia G. *Mending the Soul Workbook for Men and Women—2nd Edition* (mendingthesoul.org, 2015).

Tracy, Steven R. *Mending the Soul: Understanding and Healing Abuse.* (Grand Rapids, MI: Zondervan, 2005).

van der Kolk, Bessel. *The Body Keeps the Score: Brain, Mind, and Body in the Healing of Trauma.* (New York: Penguin Books, 2014).

Vernick, Leslie. *The Emotionally Destructive Relationship: Seeing It, Stopping It, Surviving It.* (Wheaton, IL: Harvest House Publishers 2007).

Vernick, Leslie. *The Emotionally Destructive Marriage: How to Find Your Voice and Reclaim Your Hope.* (Colorado Springs: WaterBrook Press, 2013).

8

From Abuser to Servant

The goal in handling dragons is not to destroy them, not merely to disassociate from them, but to make them disciples. Even when that seems an unlikely prospect.—Marshall Shelley[1]

Whoever says to the wicked, 'You are in the right,' will be cursed by peoples, abhorred by nations, but those who rebuke the wicked will have delight, and a good blessing will come upon them. (Prov. 24:24-25)

In Chapter 2, we described abuse as corrupt perception resulting in corrupt patterns of behavior. We said that abuse has as much to do with *who a person is* as it does with *what a person does*. Thus, heart transformation for an abusive person

---

1. Marshall Shelley, *Ministering to Problem People in the Church* (Bloomington, MN: Bethany House Publishers, 2013), 39.

involves helping him to change his ways of perceiving as much as his ways of behaving. Behavioral change is a short-term win that we will gladly take because it reduces the risk of someone being harmed, or even killed. And that is a righteous goal. Long-term transformation of an abusive heart, however, only occurs when the abuser's corrupted perceptions change. Both behavioral change and perceptual change are important, and should be pursued in tandem. The diagram below illustrates some typical categories of corrupt perception and behavior in abusers.

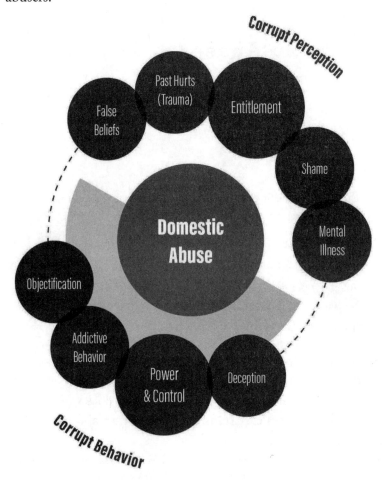

In this chapter, our goal is to help you—the pastor, church leader, counselor, or caring friend—operate as part of a team to care for an abuser as he walks out repentance, if he is willing, toward the end of becoming a servant and a person of peace.[2] There are no guarantees of success and the work is hard and frustrating. It can also be dangerous. Proceed with caution and, as always, with the advice and consent of the victim who knows him best. Remember that he will put his best foot forward for you. Even when he is responding with hostility and combativeness, you are still likely getting a toned-down version of what is witnessed in the home. Ask yourself, 'If he is responding this defensively to me, how must he be responding behind closed doors?'

The Starting Point: Assessing for Risk and Openness to Change

Because relational abuse is so devastating, we must hope for and encourage both behavioral and heart change. In biblical terms, this change is called *repentance*. In this chapter, we are proposing an approach to help a willing person repent of his abuse and pursue a more peaceful course. In Chapter 5, we outlined a range of responses you may receive, from some openness to change, to some level of ambivalence (reluctance or resistance), to hostility.

---

2. We do feel compelled to offer a strong caution here. Though we have given this chapter the hopeful title of 'From Abuser to Servant,' we want you to know that the statistics are far less hopeful. We are certain that God desires that every abuser become a servant, and our hope is in Him. We want to desire what God desires. We also know that only God can bring the kind of heart transformation that we are describing in this chapter. Sadly, most abusive men do not change, for a variety of reasons that we will discuss. Therefore, we warn you to enter this work prayerfully, and with sobriety. Continue to keep the safety of the victim(s) at the forefront of your mind as you correct perpetrators.

Hostile	Reluctance or Resistance	Open
This person exhibits the same destructive behavior towards you that he exhibits towards his spouse.	This person demonstrates reluctance (passive) or resistance (active) to change. He's not abusive towards you. He just thinks you're wrong.	This person appears open to change, at least initially. He exhibits a willingness to see and own his abuse.

On what basis is this judgment made? We suggest that the best judgments in cases of domestic abuse should be viewed as a table with three legs. Any one of these legs is not enough to support the table, but we do offer this list in prioritized fashion:

1. The victim's testimony of the person behind closed doors.[3]

2. Knowledge of how abusers operate, understood from a biblical framework that takes sin and its dynamics seriously.[4]

3. Your personal experience of the abuser's response.

Due diligence with the first two items will help improve the reliability of the third. Your personal experience of his behavior should always be informed by the victim's testimony and by a knowledge of the dynamics of relational abuse. The prior chapters were our attempt to equip you with the first two factors. Here is some guidance on the third. We will start with a visual overview, then describe it below.

---

3. The victim's testimony should be the pre-eminent basis upon which judgments are made regarding an abuser. She lives with him and knows him best. She, alone or with any children they may have, knows best what he is capable of and what happens 'behind closed doors.' You create danger for her if you minimize or dismiss her perspective of him.

4. Chapters 2-3 were our attempt to offer such a framework.

Initial Response	Recommended Approach to Care
Hostile: This person exhibits abusive behavior toward you: threats, bullying, manipulation, gaslighting, etc. His behavior toward you will validate his wife's experiences.	• Safety of the victim(s) is always the first priority. • Follow safety plan to protect victim(s). • If hostility continues, follow a church discipline plan related to outrageous public sins (1 Cor. 5). • Don't feel obligated to offer him care if he will not follow recommendations or is unsafe. • Suggest a professional counselor and/or batterer intervention group program.
Reluctant or Resistant: This person demonstrates reluctant (passive) or resistant (active) ambivalence to change. He's not abusive toward you. He just thinks you're wrong about him or is not sure he wants to change.	• Safety of the victim(s) is still your utmost priority. • If resistance continues, follow a church discipline plan related to gradual confrontation of sin patterns (Matt. 18). • If he will submit to pastoral care, suggest counseling with a counselor experienced in the dynamics of relational abuse. Counseling should be focused on helping him understand how both his perception and his behaviors have been corrupted. It should also invite him into a process of repentance and amends that will take time. • Consider asking him to participate in a batterer intervention group or *Men of Peace* program.

Open: This person appears open to change, at least initially. He exhibits a willingness to see and own his abuse.	• Safety of the victim(s) remains the first priority. • Remember that change becomes reliable only when proven over time in new patterns. • Suggest counseling with a counselor experienced in the dynamics of relational abuse. Counseling should be focused on helping him understand how both his perception and his behaviors have been corrupted. It should also invite him into a process of repentance and amends that will take time. • Consider asking him to participate in a batterer intervention group or *Men of Peace* program.

Hostile

A hostile response may be expressed in an aggressive, overt way or in a cold, cutting way. The main indicator of a hostile response is not the emotional temperature of his response, but how immovable he is in his perspective and how opposed he is to anyone challenging it. He may concede that his behavior is not ideal, but he opposes any consequences that would be in keeping with how serious it actually is. If he responds with hostility to confrontation by a church leader or elder, how much worse might his responses be in private? This should be cause for concern.

Recommended Approach:

1. **Safety.** The only church-based intervention available when an abuser is hostile is to protect the victim(s) and, by extension, the church.[5] Make sure that a safety plan is in place, revise it if necessary, and provide any assistance to the victim that you can. A hostile perpetrator is what Proverbs calls a 'scoffer.'

   > Whoever corrects a scoffer gets himself abuse, and he who reproves a wicked man incurs injury (Prov. 9:7).

2. **Church Discipline.** Hopefully your church has a process for church discipline that recognizes the need to hold members accountable for living lives that reflect hearts that have been regenerated by the Holy Spirit. Church discipline is for the good of the sinner as well as the church, and can occur as immediate removal for outrageous public sins (1 Cor. 5:1-2) or a more gradual confrontation process that may result in eventual removal (Matt. 18:15-20).[6] Whatever the

---

5. A professional can help do a risk assessment of the likelihood of a perpetrator to re-assault. Professionals often use an intimate partner violence prediction instrument such as the Danger Assessment Instrument (DAI; Jacquelyn C. Campbell and Jill Theresa Messing, *Assessing Dangerousness, Third Edition: Domestic Violence Offenders and Child Abusers*, [Thousand Oaks, CA: Sage, 1995]), the Spousal Assault Risk Assessment Guide (SARA; Philip Randall Kropp et. al., *Manual for the Spousal Assault Risk Assessment Guide*, [Vancouver, BC: British Columbia Institute Against Family Violence, 1995]), or the Partner Assault Prognostic Scale (PAPS; Christopher M. Murphy et. al., 'A Prognostic Indicator Scale for the Treatment of Domestic Abuse Perpetrators,' *Journal of Interpersonal Violence*, 18, 1087-1105) to evaluate the likelihood of danger. The Mosaic Assessment is an online tool that can also be helpful for screening (mosaicmethod.com).

6. For a helpful resource on church discipline, see Jonathan Leeman, *The Church and the Surprising Offense of God's Love: Reintroducing the Doctrines of Church Membership and Discipline* (Wheaton, IL: Crossway, 2010). See also Leeman's *Church Discipline: How the Church*

particulars of the situation, an unrepentant abuser should not be allowed to remain in the self-deception that he is in good standing before the Lord.

3. **Group Intervention Program and/or Individual Counseling.** You might suggest that the hostile abuser consider a local group-based batterer intervention and prevention program (BIPP), and/or see a local professional counselor. If the courts have been involved in the situation, the abuser may be court-ordered to participate in a BIPP. Other times, it won't be a requirement, but it still may be a good idea if the program accepts voluntary participants. The goal of such programs is usually to help abusers take responsibility for their behaviors, empathize with their victims, and develop some plan of restitution. These programs often have a lot of common sense reality that will help an abuser see himself better, but without a biblical framework for understanding sin and redemption, they cannot yield true heart change. So our advice is to use such programs as supplements to, not replacements of, heart-focused, Christ-centered counseling, where possible. Ideally you could find a Christ-centered group with these same goals but with biblical grounding, like *Men of Peace*. For more information on a local BIPP group, contact your local domestic abuse resource organization, using the state resources in Appendix C. More information is available on *Men of Peace* groups at menofpeace.org. Such a person is usually not a good candidate to follow-through voluntarily with getting help, because he doesn't believe that he needs it. However, you have provided him with a resource that

Protects the Name of Jesus (Wheaton, IL: Crossway, 2012). We also recommend Jeremy Pierre, 'An Overlooked Help: Church Discipline and the Protection of Women' in *The Journal for Biblical Manhood and Womanhood* 18 (Spring 2013), 12-15.

he may return to when he is a little more open to receiving help.

Reluctant (Passive) or Resistant (Active)

This ambivalent response is less unsettling than a hostile one, but should still be concerning to you. The way we are using these terms, *reluctance* is a passive form of ambivalence, while *resistance* is more overt, sometimes bordering on aggressive. As you dig into what is behind the reluctance by asking good questions, you will usually find that reluctance reflects fear (of vulnerability or change), shame, or distrust (of the person who is engaging him, or of the process). We encourage you to approach reluctance with a sensitivity to the fear, shame, or distrust that is being reflected. Helping him to process his fear, shame, or distrust may be a helpful step toward winning his respect and may open a window into his heart.

Resistance is usually reflected in overtly oppositional behaviors such as arguing, correcting, interrupting, minimizing, denying, or blaming. He may attempt to downplay the abuse, 'I know I'm harsh with her, but I am not abusive,' or 'I'm not as bad as you seem to think I am.' Sometimes he will attempt to shift the blame, 'If anyone is being abused in the relationship, it's me,' or 'You do know my wife struggles with mental illness, right?' Sometimes he will attempt to wrangle about definitions, 'I want to know your exact definition of abuse,' or 'Why is your understanding of abuse the right one?' Sometimes he will attempt to argue from his understanding of Scripture, 'Why aren't you acknowledging what the Bible says about a wife submitting to her husband?' or 'This whole time I've been guilty until proven innocent—what happened to admitting a charge only with two or three witnesses?' We usually recommend respecting the resistance and going with it, rather than against it. Getting into an argument with him about his behavior will be a dead end. Instead, you should listen to him, express empathy, labor to understand his concerns, find the discrepancy between his expressed concerns and his behavior, and try to determine if he even has any interest in change.

Recommended Approach:

1. **Safety.** Since the abuser is ambivalent to recognizing his perceptions and behaviors as abusive, he still poses a threat to his victim(s). Make sure that a safety plan is in place, revise it if necessary, and provide any necessary assistance to the victim.

2. **Pastoral Care.** In our experience, you are more likely to encounter an ambivalent response than either a hostile or open response initially. As indicated above, reluctance or resistance doesn't have to be a roadblock. Seeking to understand what is operating behind his reluctance or resistance can provide helpful pastoral insight.

   Pastoral care here is patient, unyielding effort to help him see his sin, without getting into arguments with him that will be non-productive and could create a safety concern. You are essentially following a Matthew 18 model for church discipline, related to gradual confrontation of sin patterns. Make sure that you follow our suggestions for a coordinated community response to care through a team-based approach later in this chapter.

3. **Group Intervention Program and/or Individual Counseling.** We recommend suggesting he consider voluntary participation in a local batterer intervention and prevention program (BIPP), if your local program accepts voluntary participants. Appendix C will provide you with

some national and local resources to help you locate such a program. We also believe that individual counseling with a counselor experienced in the dynamics of relational abuse can help him understand how both his perception and behavior have been corrupted. A Christ-centered counselor who has a good understanding of the dynamics we've discussed in Section 1 of this book may be a great asset to the church in inviting the abuser into a process of repentance that does not too quickly try to make amends, which can threaten true change.

Some professional counselors will be open to working with the church, as long as their client is open to providing a release of information.

Open

An open response is characterized by a person's apparent willingness to acknowledge his behavior as abusive. He may express a desire to change. Further, he may seem to emotionally register the weight of the damage he has caused to others as his motivation for change. He may even make statements acknowledging responsibility for his actions. In other words, he appears to be submissive to a process he's not controlling, one that prioritizes his wife's concerns over his own.

Encountering such an open response initially is rare in our experience. At least, in an ongoing way that validates the legitimacy of his openness. An individual may appear ready, sometimes even hungry, to engage with the process. He may devour teaching, request discipleship, and attend any group, program, or counseling that is asked of him. He may respond with appropriate sadness for what he has done and the hurt he has caused. But you cannot conclude—nor should he or anyone else—that his repentance is genuine at this point. Genuine repentance is characterized by decisive change (2 Cor. 7:10-11), and turning from an established pattern of harmful sin requires the time to establish new patterns of selflessness and humility.

Recommended Approach:

1. **Safety.** Our advice, then, is not to conclude early that he is repentant or that his motives are pure. Remember, abusers do what they do because they want something. His eagerness may wane when he realizes it isn't necessarily going to gain him anything in the short term. At the point that he sees that he still may lose his marriage or his status in the church, he may even become ambivalent, or even hostile, thereby demonstrating that his sorrow was worldly (based on what he has lost) and not godly (based on what he has done). It is still wise to maintain a safety plan, revise it if necessary, and be alert to any safety concerns that may arise.

2. **Pastoral Care.** A biblically robust understanding of sin means we have to be willing to avoid trusting someone that has not demonstrated himself trustworthy—especially when the issue is his trustworthiness with vulnerable people. Solomon's wisdom with people teaches us this, 'Whoever hates disguises himself with his lips and harbors deceit in his heart; when he speaks graciously, *believe him not*, for there are seven abominations in his heart; though his hatred be covered with deception, his wickedness will be exposed in the assembly' (Prov. 26:24-26, italics added). However, we also advise you to avoid concluding prematurely that his openness is fake. Healthy skepticism should not devolve into complete mistrust without demonstrated reason. Wait for the fruit of change with hope, but realism. You can encourage the person by pointing out that he has evidenced a desire to engage with the process of repentance, and this

is the starting point that leads to good fruit. Make sure that you continue to follow our suggestions for a coordinated community response to care through a team-based approach later in this chapter. Wise care for him in the church will be patiently leading him through the repentance and reconciliation process described later in this chapter.

3. **Group Intervention Program and/or Individual Counseling.** Participation in a BIPP or *Men of Peace* men's group intervention program, as described above can always be a wise aspect for care. Men who are open to seeing and owning their abuse may even be an encouragement to men who aren't as receptive to change. Likewise, individual counseling is also recommended for men at all levels of openness to change.

Now that we've addressed different starting points, let's consider the team that will journey along with you in helping.

The Team: Others You Need on the Journey

You can't help an abuser on this journey alone. You need the wisdom, availability, and vigilance of others beyond you. Besides, it's been largely established in domestic abuse literature that team-based interventions have the greatest chance of long-term success.[7] This makes sense, given the biblical idea

---

7. See the following resources for research on coordinated community response and team-based interventions for abusers: Edward W. Gondolf, *The Future of Batterer Programs* (Boston: Northeastern University Press, 2012), Edward W. Gondolf, *Batterer Intervention Systems: Issues, Outcomes, and Recommendations* (Thousand Oaks, CA: Sage Publications, 2002), Ellen Pence, 'Batterer Programs: Shifting from Community Collusion to Community Confrontation,' in *Treating Men Who Batter: Theory, Practice, and Programs*, edited by P. Lynn Caesar and L. Kevin Hamberger, 24-50 (New York:

of formation in the community of faith (Eph. 4:13). What we will suggest in this section is an approach that's orchestrated by church leaders making wise use of the resources available to them.

As displayed in the diagram below, we suggest a three-part team in close communication with one another to help an abuser change. The first part is the Shepherding Team, which consists of the appointed individuals in the church most involved in helping the abuser. The second part is the counselor or group program overseeing an abuser's progress in changing his perspective and behaviors. The third part is the victim's counselor or advocate, who keeps the interests of the victim informing the process. We call this concept *360 degree accountability*. Let's look a little closer at these three components.

Springer, 1989), Ellen Pence and Michael Paymar, *Education Groups for Men Who Batter: The Duluth Model* (New York: Springer, 1993), and Christopher M. Murphy et. al., 'Coordinated Community Intervention for Domestic Abusers: Intervention System Involvement and Criminal Recidivism,' *Journal of Family Violence*, 13, 263-84.

- **Victim's Counselor and/or Advocate.** In the previous chapter on helping victims overcome, we already mentioned the need for counseling. But helping her process her concerns in counseling is only part of the strategy. You also have to represent her concerns in the larger process. This is why we suggest that the victim's counselor *or* a trained lay victim advocate[8] communicate with church leadership to speak into the direction of guidance for the abuser. As we have already discussed, the abuser's perception of reality is corrupted and cannot be trusted, regardless of however loved and respected he may be in the church. When the voice of the abused individual is not present, care for the abuser can turn into inadvertent collusion.

- **Abuser's Counselor and/or Group Program.** The counselor's job is to guide an abuser on the difficult journey of recognizing the heart issues that led to abuse—the false beliefs, the motivating desires, the skewed commitments. Part of recognizing these heart issues will involve considering the contextual influences and co-occurring issues that shaped these wrong ideas and deceitful desires, including factors such as entitlement, shame, cognitive distortions, past trauma, and co-occurring mental health disorders. A counselor with specialized training or experience working with abusers becomes more urgent the more entrenched a person is in their corrupted perceptions and behaviors.[9]

---

8. In Appendix E, we provide a role description for a church care advocate. Churches seeking to be prepared to address domestic abuse should consider training care advocates specifically for this role. Victim advocacy training programs such as Joy Forrest's Called to Peace Ministries can be quite helpful in giving direction to your church's training.

9. In Appendix C, we offer a short guide to finding competent domestic violence resources in your local area or making use of group programs designed to help abusers understand the dynamics of their abuse.

- **Shepherding and Accountability Team.** In Chapter 5, we encouraged you to form this team to hold the abuser accountable and to shepherd him through the repentance and amends process. This could include his pastor, an elder, church staff member, deacon, care advocate as defined in Appendix E, or other faithful brothers or sisters in the church. As displayed in the diagram, the shepherding team coordinates the overall spiritual care of the abuser, while utilizing the expertise and insights of the different counselors involved. Humble dialogue is essential for this, characterized by pastors being willing both to adjust their approach according to the advice of experts and to take responsibility for ensuring that biblical principles of accountability and discipleship guide the process. The shepherding team's goal is to help the abuser repent of his abuse. This involves leading him to see, to own, to hate, and to turn from his sin. The next section describes this process.

Communication between these parties is critical to a team-based approach, as represented by the arrows. For this reason, the shepherding team should ask the abuser to sign release of information consents from any professional counselor or intervention program involved in the process.[10]

Group programs like Chris Moles' *Men of Peace* coach men who wish to take responsibility for the abusive patterns that characterize them.

10. Releases of Information (ROIs) are vital to obtain in order to coordinate. Because confidentiality is critical to the professional relationship, professional clinicians (marriage and family therapists, social workers, counselors, psychologists, and psychiatrists) will not release any information about their clients (even their names or the fact that they have a professional relationship with the person) to an outside party without a formal, written, and signed release of information. The client, who in the context of this chapter is the abuser, is the one agreeing that the professional can release their protected health information (PHI) to another party. This agreement is at the

This may seem like too large a team for your church or community. We realize that church sizes and community resources will vary greatly by location. At a minimum, we suggest one trained individual caring for the victim, one trained individual or group working with the perpetrator, and one pastor or church leader providing spiritual oversight. However, larger teams than that are definitely ideal.

The Process: Repentance and Reconciliation with God

We covered how to determine a starting point as well as a team to help, but what is the process of change? How do we understand progress in an abuser's life?

The key word is *repentance*. But don't think of repentance in one-dimensional terms—as if it's simply admitting sin or even saying sorry for it. Repentance is a deep, even brutal, change in a person's heart caused by the Lord Himself. It demolishes established patterns of response, patterns that involve internal ways of seeing as much as external ways of behaving. Repentance is disruptive and painful, and therefore often inhibited by a number of underlying issues. A trained counselor with knowledge of abuse dynamics can help give

---

client's discretion. You should never attempt to require or coerce the client/patient to sign an ROI for you. As mentioned above, we believe that the process can be enhanced if the counselors and advocates for the perpetrator and victim are able to talk to each other—primarily so that they can be on the same page and not be giving conflicting counsel. However, the client's PHI is protected under the U.S. Health Insurance Portability and Accountability Act (HIPAA). You don't want to infringe on anyone's right to determine who has access to that information and who does not. If the abuser is resistant to signing, do not give him an ultimatum; instead explain to him the importance of coordinated care and tell him that you don't feel you can responsibly oversee the process without the proper ROIs.

insight into those issues; the shepherding team's job is to help an abuser process these issues through the central consideration of *his heart in relation to God*. Repentance is a holistic turn away from self and toward God. As a person turns toward God, he becomes more like Him.

This deep change is a process involving *seeing, owning, hating,* and *turning*.

It begins with *seeing* for himself the destructive patterns of his own thinking and behaving. Seeing his sin is the growing acknowledgement that the behavior patterns actually exist and that they are actually destructive.

It leads to *owning* the patterns of destruction as his own personal fault that he is responsible for. In order to own his sin, the abuser must learn to move past the typical defensive strategies of minimizing it, denying it, or blaming it on the victim or someone else. Owning means he will be able to recognize genuine difficulties he has faced, but not label them the cause of his own behaviors.

This develops into *hating* these patterns because they are morally ugly and wicked in the eyes of God. As an abuser submits his perspective to God's, he will start to feel toward abuse what God feels toward abuse: hatred. This hatred is not self-indulgent flagellation, but a sober, fearful realization of the cruelty he'd become capable of.

It also results in a decisive *turning* from these patterns with a kind of reverse violence against his sin. True repentance is only revealed by consistent change over a long period of time. Abusive patterns will have to be broken. New patterns of behavior will need to be developed. All of this takes time. Only genuine heart change, resulting in fruit-bearing repentance, can interrupt these patterns of abuse.

We put the repentance process at the center of the diagram on pages 194-195 to emphasize its centrality in all of the potential complexities contributing to the abuser's pattern of response.

In our experience, most perpetrators of domestic abuse come for help when they realize that their abuse is no longer working for them. Their grief is related to what they have lost or may lose. This is usually the relationship; however, they may face other potential losses as well—access to their children, personal reputation, control of his situation, and more. What they usually want when they come for help is to protect or regain those things. While this remorse is not entirely wrong, it is entirely deficient as a motivator for true change. Mere remorse is a form of what Scripture calls a 'worldly sorrow.' It is grief over what a person has lost. Repentance is what Scripture calls 'godly sorrow' – it is grief over what a person has *done.*

> As it is, I rejoice, not because you were grieved, but because you were grieved into repenting. For you felt a godly grief, so that you suffered no loss through us. For godly grief produces a repentance that leads to salvation without regret, whereas worldly grief produces death (2 Cor. 7:9-10).

The goal is to challenge him beyond remorse to repentance. You will be leading him to focus on the harm he has caused more than the benefits he has lost. The most pressing loss in his mind will likely be his marriage. Even if there is not separation or divorce, he will likely want to get back to normal as soon as possible. No one wants his life disrupted. But reconciling the marriage cannot be the initial focus. In fact, doing so undermines the greater priority on not just the safety of the victim but also the state of the abuser's soul before a holy God.

We'd like to make one other note about the distinction between remorse and repentance that is particularly pertinent to abusers. The line between remorse and repentance is perhaps most blurry when he is expressing regret over himself and even his behavior. What may on the face of things look like repentance may just be frustration with himself for not being a better person. In other words, the good he lost was self-respect, and he wants to get it back. He doesn't want to acknowledge how desperately sinful he'd allowed himself to become. He holds on to the assumption that he should be a better person than that, and hates himself for becoming 'that kind of guy.' But a bruised ego is not repentance.

This process focuses on the harm the abuser has caused more than the benefits he lost; more on the unreliability of his own perspective more than on his right to 'tell his side'; more on the offense of his unrighteous leadership than on his frustrations with her lack of following. This may sound unfair to him, but it is not. It is the only path back to God and the true forgiveness He offers. Until a perpetrator is truly repentant for what he has done, not just sorry for what he has lost, there will be no trustworthy change.

Does He SEE His Behavior Patterns as Abusive?

For any lasting change to take place, the abuser must first see his sin. As we have already noted, abusive people typically lack self-awareness due to the hardening effect of sin (Heb. 3:12-13; 1 John 1:8-10). The first and perhaps hardest obstacle to repentance is a person seeing his sin the way God sees it.

To help him see his sin, you have to venture into the specifics. There's just no other way. It's far more comfortable to stay in generalities. But staying in generalities does not serve anyone well in situations like this. Remember, you are addressing both patterns of corrupted behavior as well as a corrupted mindset. Specifics are the only way to help someone see how skewed their perspective has become.

As you get into specifics, we would reiterate the need to avoid unhelpful arguments over terminology. If the term *abuse* or *abusive* brings too much initial resistance, it's okay to refer to these patterns as *destructive, mean, cruel,* or *harmful* for now. All of these words describe the antithesis of how a Christian man should treat those he's called to love sacrificially.

The abuser's counselor or group program will, ideally, be trained to help him take an inventory of all of the ways he has hurt his partner (and others in his life) through the misuse of power and control. You should help with this process by asking into the specifics of how he speaks to his wife, how he acts toward her physically, how he approaches her sexually, how money is used between them, and how he talks about God, Scripture, spirituality, and authority.

These are obviously uncomfortable conversations, but you are trying to help him recognize his sin specifically. This is where communication with the victim or those caring for her can be helpful. You may need to start with a list of the abusive behaviors that the victim has reported to those who are caring for her. Obviously, wisdom and care should be exercised regarding how to use this list of abusive behaviors in working with the abuser. In some cases, it may be shared with the abuser with the advice/consent of the victim. In most cases, it is simply used to inform those counseling the abuser and holding him accountable, so that they know what they are looking for.

It is generally nonproductive and unhelpful for the abuser to acknowledge his abuse to his spouse initially. Because repentance is more shown than told, and showing happens over time as appropriate contact is established, not much is gained by too quick of an acknowledgement. As an abusive husband grows in his own understanding of his sin, his verbal acknowledgement will be more mature, thorough, and forthright. That will serve

From Abuser to Servant

Seeing

I am increasingly self-aware.

I do whatever is necessary to facilitate healing for the trauma I have caused.

I submit to rigorous accountability.

I confess the weight and impact of my abuse on my spouse and family (trauma).

I refuse to make excuses for my abuse.

I refuse to deny my abuse.

I agree that I have hurt my spouse and others in specific ways – and name them.

I see how my past hurts are affecting my present behavior.

I see how I may have been socialized or discipled into some unhealthy ways of relating.

I see how I have objectified my spouse (and others) instead of valuing as an image-bearer.

I refuse to lie, hide, or deceive.

I walk with others who can help me continue to see specifically and make specific changes.

I refuse to mutualize my abuse.

I desire self-awareness for myself and empathy for others.

I educate myself about abuse dynamics.

I examine my core entitlements and ask others to help me examine them.

I recognize that it takes time for my repentant heart to bear fruit and I practice patience with timetables.

I am perceived as increasingly safe by my spouse and my family.

I live out of my identity as an image-bearer of God (and, if a believer, as a child of God.)

I serve my wife and family selflessly, rather than controlling them.

I treat with respect those I formerly harmed.

I make specific amends for the ways in which I have hurt my spouse and family.

I am more self-controlled, less impulsive.

I do whatever it takes to provide for the safety and security of my spouse and my family.

I embrace ongoing accountability.

I refuse to minimize the ways I have hurt my spouse and others.

I am more vulnerable, less self-protective.

I become a fierce advocate of my spouse and family, as well as others who have experienced abuse.

I reject my core entitlements and pursue the mind of Christ.

I refuse to blame my abuse on others or outside circumstances.

Owning | Hating | Turning

I grow in vulnerability about my own biases and knowledge gaps.

I call out abuse wherever I see it because I have seen first-hand the damage it does.

I use my power, position, and authority to serve others, rather than to get what I want.

I work on my own past hurts so that I won't continue to hurt others.

I catch myself when I fall back into abusive patterns.

I am less controlled by my sin, suffering, and brokenness and more controlled by the love of Christ.

I pursue reconciliation with the Lord before reconciliation with my spouse and family.

I examine my own perceptions and misperceptions and ask others to call them out.

I demonstrate an eagerness to serve my spouse and my children.

I am demonstrating fewer destructive patterns of behavior and more peaceful patterns of behavior.

a victim far more than a hasty, half-baked acknowledgement early on.

As shown in the diagram on pages 194-195, progress in seeing his abuse will be demonstrated as he is able to name specific ways that he has hurt his spouse and others. He should be able to recognize how any past abuse, abandonment, loss, or betrayal may be affecting his present behavior. Since power and control is a common dynamic in abuse, he should be able to see where he has exercised power over the other person to get what he wants. He should be able to see how he has objectified others, rather than valuing them as fellow image-bearers of God. He should at least exhibit a desire to gain further self-awareness for himself and empathy for others. And he should be open to further accountability and insights from your team and others.

Practical Strategy: Ask the husband what word he would use to describe the patterns of behavior that his wife has found unsafe, hurtful, or destructive. You are helping him acknowledge specific sins and the hurt those sins have caused. You start generally and move toward the specific details.

For example, you might ask, 'What word would you use to describe a pattern of repeatedly putting down your wife and calling her names?' We have heard responses such as, 'I would call that mean, but not abusive.' You can then respond with, 'Then let's discuss the specifics of your mean behavior toward your wife. In what other ways have you been mean to her?' In any case, the outcome you are looking for is a specific list of abusive, hurtful, destructive, mean, cruel, harmful, or corrupt behaviors that the abuser acknowledges he has committed. This includes getting to the specifics like, 'What demeaning terms have you used? What names have you called her? How many times? When was the last time? When was the time prior to that? About how often? How do you act when she doesn't do what you're wanting her to?'

Deliverable: For each of these items, we will include a tangible, deliverable item for the husband to help produce throughout this process. For this initial stage of helping him to see his sin, work with him to create an Inventory of Abusive Behaviors. (If he is unwilling to use the word abuse yet, he may be more agreeable to the exercise if you call it Inventory of Harmful Behaviors. But this adjustment should not alter the moral clarity you are bringing to his behaviors.) This should be a comprehensive list of behaviors that he committed that had harmful, diminishing effects on his spouse.

Can He OWN His Abuse Without Minimizing, Denying, or Blaming?

It is not enough that the abusive person acknowledges his sin. He must also own it. Owning his sin means taking sole responsibility for his sinful responses, both in attitude and in action. It means refusing to minimize, deny, and blame others for his own sinful way of seeing others and his own actions toward them. Domestic violence interventionists learn to be alert to these 'big three' common defenses that keep perpetrators from owning their abuse. We will add a fourth: redefining intentionality.

* Minimization is belittling the victim's experience of harm from the abuser's actions. For example: 'At least I didn't (fill-in-the-blank with something worse) to her,' or 'I just pushed her.'

* Denial is undermining the victim's perspective of reality by stating or implying that it didn't happen. For example: 'What she's saying happened simply did not happen,' or, 'I do not remember the event she's telling you about at all.'

- Blame is assigning fault to the victim for the harm she experienced. For example: 'She spit at me, so I had to grab her,' or, 'I was worried she'd harm herself or the kids, so I had to take matters into my own hands.'

- Redefining intentionality is defending his conduct because his actions did not intend harm. This defensive strategy is tricky, because it defines intentionality solely according to a conscious purpose to harm. But this is a shallow understanding of intentionality. A person can intend to get his own way, and forcefulness is his means of ensuring he gets it.[11] In that case, an abuser can think himself innocent because he didn't directly intend harm; however, his commitment to his own will drove him to act harmfully. Here are examples of what you might hear from him: 'I would never intentionally harm her,' or 'You're acting like I want to abuse my wife, and I don't.'

---

11. Pastor and domestic abuse expert Al Miles claimed that every pastor needs to know that domestic abuse 'is caused by the conscious decision and willful choice of perpetrators to use abusive tactics.' (*Domestic Violence: What Every Pastor Needs to Know* [Minneapolis: Fortress Press], 3). Ellen Pence, co-founder of Minnesota's nationally-recognized Duluth Domestic Abuse Intervention Project, agrees. Pence asserts that abusive behaviors are not unintentional, but that each abusive act can be traced back to an intention of the abuser's. (Ellen Pence, 'Batterer Programs: Shifting from Community Collusion to Community Confrontation,' in *Treating Men Who Batter: Theory, Practice, and Programs*, ed. P. Lynn Caesar and L. Kevin Hamberger [New York: Springer Publishing, 1989], 36.) Consider from Psalm 10 how the oppressor 'hotly pursues' (2a), devises 'schemes' (2b), and 'sits in ambush' (8a). His eyes 'stealthily watch' for the helpless (8c). He 'lurks in ambush' that he may seize the poor; he 'seizes the poor when he draws them into his net' (9). Elsewhere in Scripture, abusive people 'devise wrongs' (Ps 58:2) and their hearts 'devise violence' (Prov 24:2). The heart of an abusive person devises and executes violence with intentionality. In the words of David Powlison, 'People think about using and abusing others. Violence and betrayal are not accidental but devised.' (David Powlison, 'Predator, Prey, and Protector: Helping Victims Think and Act from Psalm 10,' *Journal of Biblical Counseling*)

These defenses become so integrated into the abuser's tactical repertoire that they actually become an extension of the abuse and help sustain it. The abuser can minimize his abuse enough that the victim may even feel bad about being so sensitive. He can deny it to the point that the victim believes she is crazy for believing that the abuse actually happened. This is commonly called *gaslighting*. His victim-blaming behavior can lead to the victim actually believing the abuse is her fault.

Walking with an abuser through the repentance process will require you to point out these defenses and how they keep him from owning his harmful behaviors. Minimization, denial, and blame are accountability blockers. Perpetrators of abuse who genuinely desire accountability will exhibit an increasing desire to learn how they are impeding accountability so that they can stop being abusive.

Practical Strategy: Help them recognize minimizing, denying, or blaming statements by asking them why they describe their responses the way they do.

For minimizing, ask him why he used terms like only, just, at least, or I could have as they describe their behaviors. What do these terms show about his perspective of the seriousness of the offense? Would God use the same words to describe these sins?

For denying, ask him if he thinks the victim completely made up the situation or if there is some kernel of truth she's exaggerating or otherwise misrepresenting? Ask him if a person being harmed or a person doing the harming would be more likely to remember the situation correctly, and why?

For blaming, ask him how the victim's actions make his actions acceptable before God. Would you advise someone with a wife like yours to take those same actions toward her?

For redefining intentionality, you can have two approaches: First, ask him if an action can have unintended consequences—

like a person driving drunk not intending to kill someone. Is a person responsible for unintended consequences? Second, point out that all actions have intention behind them, so what was his intention in the way he treated his wife? Does the Lord agree that harm is justifiable to fulfill that intention?

We will often go back to the original acknowledgement of specific sins and patterns with the abuser and ask him to look for and edit statements or phrases that minimize, deny, or blame. To the inventory that was created earlier, the abuser may add ways that he has blocked accountability for these behaviors and patterns by refusing to own them in the past.

Deliverable: For helping him move beyond seeing to actually owning, the next step with the Inventory of Abusive Behaviors is to work together to write for each item on the list a description of the heart attitude that led to the behavior. By heart attitude, we mean the beliefs, desires, or commitments that motivated him to act the way he did. What did this behavior show he was wanting from her? What does God think of that desire? Or, what did this behavior show he was believing about himself, about her, or failing to believe about God? What was the greatest commitment of his heart in the moment he chose to take the action he did?

A person accepting responsibility for his abusive behaviors does not happen in a movie-like moment of clarity. It usually happens gradually, with clearer and clearer willingness to name his behavior as abusive. This means he is starting to give up minimizing, denying, or blaming the victim. He is with greater precision acknowledging that his commitment to getting his own way has harmed his wife. It is appropriate to celebrate this milestone and then press on to the necessary work of hating and turning from abusive behavior patterns. He may have a long way to go before being trustworthy enough for reunification, but you can still recognize the Holy Spirit's gradual work in him. Relapse into old patterns is not just possible, but likely. But the key is continuing to be alert to seeing and owning those patterns when they return, quickly accepting responsibility as he has before, and continuing on in the process of repentance. It is also important to remind the victim that repentance is a process. We are looking for progress, not perfection, in the development of new behavior patterns.[12]

Is He Growing in HATE Toward His Abusive Patterns?

Hate is a powerful motivation. We typically use this word negatively, since we think of hate as the opposite of love. But hate can be a positive force when directed at what is hateworthy. God hates abuse, and as a man gradually submits his perspective to God's, he will start to hate it too. If a man has endured through the process thus far, there ought to be signs of this growing hatred, specifically for what he has done and who he had become. Despising sin is critical to change.

---

12. It's not unusual for the shepherding team to become fatigued by the process somewhere around this point. As weariness sets in, a few reminders may be helpful: (1) The abusive behavior patterns probably have been in place much longer than it has taken to get to this point of accepting responsibility for them. (2) We should not expect recovery from abusive behavior patterns to be a quick process. (3) The abuser has probably apologized many times before, but then continued in the abusive patterns. Press him with the gospel promise that this time can be different. (4) The hard work of developing new, peaceful, non-abusive patterns of behavior is where the real benefit is, both for the abuser and for the victim. That work is still to come.

Though it isn't ideal, you may have to make some adjustments to the shepherding team due to fatigue or other interpersonal reasons. Fatigue is an understandable part of suffering alongside a brother through a long, difficult process. You may at this point re-evaluate the commitments of the folks who are involved, encouraging them to rededicate themselves to this good, long work.

Jesus uses unsettling language to help us understand the imperative of hating our sin and anything that provokes that sin in us.

> And if your hand or your foot causes you to sin, cut it off and throw it away. It is better for you to enter life crippled or lame than with two hands or two feet to be thrown into the eternal fire. And if your eye causes you to sin, tear it out and throw it away. It is better for you to enter life with one eye than with two eyes to be thrown into the hell of fire (Matt. 18:8-9).

Jesus uses the hyperbolic idea of self-mutilation to show how extreme our hatred of sin should be. We should despise even our most useful and beloved body parts—hands, feet, eyes—if they put us in the eternal danger of continued sin. The apostle Paul uses the language of fleeing from sin (1 Cor. 6:18 and 10:14; 1 Tim. 6:11 and 2 Tim. 2:22) and putting it to death (Col. 3:5). Our revulsion for sin leads us to turn from it.

You can't make someone else's heart love or hate the right things. What a person loves and hates will be displayed by the direction he takes in relation to those objects. So what you can do is point out what the right love and hate will look like practically in his life.

Hatred for abuse will be displayed most clearly in the way they speak to God about their sin and the way they speak to others about it. Specifically, he will (1) lament his sin before God and (2) accept the consequences of his harmful behaviors before others, making genuine amends that are not on his own terms with everyone he has harmed.

Lamenting is the long outpouring of regret before the Lord that began with his initial confession. Confession of sin, as you'll recall, is agreeing with God about the offense of his sin and asking forgiveness for it (1 John 1:8-10). That is not a one-time interaction, but an ongoing realization of how destructive, ugly, and worthy of condemnation personal sin is. This deepening understanding results in crying out to Jesus Christ as the only one who can both forgive and cleanse a man for his sin.

Accepting consequences for harmful behaviors means submitting to what he can't control. He will acknowledge that others have had to respond to the residue of his sin in the best ways they can, and submit to their responses. If he hates his sin more than he hates the pain of its consequences, he will not be hostile when things don't go his way. He will stop seeking to repair his reputation with everyone. He will stop trying to coerce people to respond with less consequences. He will even be willing to face with dignity the possibility that his marriage is ending.

Recognizing the impact his sin has caused makes it possible for him to make genuine amends with those he has harmed that are not based on his own terms. Making amends like this means he is listening to how others describe the wrong he has done, then seeking to make it right on their terms and on the Bible's terms. He displays a heart like the repentant Zacchaeus' when he says, 'Behold, Lord, the half of my goods I give to the poor. And if I have defrauded anyone of anything, I restore it fourfold' (Luke 19:8). Zacchaeus was motivated to restore with interest the money he had defrauded people of, presumably emptying himself of the wealth he had accumulated for so long. Jesus confirms this as a fruit of salvation.

This principle can be displayed in abusive situations in a variety of ways:

- An abuser who has demeaned his wife in front of their children should go to each child to confess what he has done as sin and give them permission to call him out if he ever speaks ill of their mother again.

- An abuser who has tried to destroy his wife's reputation with friends or relatives should go to each one to confess this as sin. He may even go further and tell them about the godly qualities he sees in her that he has previously tried to hide from them.

- An abuser who has cut his wife off financially in some way should be willing to restore mutuality to their finances.

- An abuser who has been hiding his pornography use from his wife or gaslighting her about it should confess the full extent of it and acknowledge that he had been deceiving her. He should ask for her forgiveness and express his commitment to transparency and change.

In making amends, the abusive person is demonstrating a desire to change and making the important turn toward bearing fruit of repentance. This part of the process is sometimes awkward and clumsy at first. Give grace and lots of room for trial and error in the amends process, as this begins to form the template for turning from abusive patterns. Pray with him for change resulting from the kind of effort driven by grace and not by fear or shame.

> *Practical Strategy: You are guiding a man through the process of (1) lamenting his sin before God and (2) accepting the consequences of his harmful behaviors before others by making amends with them on their terms, not his.*
>
> *For lamenting, you are likely at a place where he has already confessed his sin but is still learning to hate it. He is still learning to be moved with aversion for what he has done. You must keep in mind that even for such deeply shameful sins as abuse, shame will not produce the right kind of hatred. Grace will.*

Grace allows us to acknowledge both the deep shamefulness of personal sin and the hope that personal identity is not ultimately tied to that shame. Keep both in mind as you address his sin. For instance, in 1 Timothy 1:12-17, Paul is very honest about the abhorrent sins of his past, even twice declaring himself the 'foremost' of sinners. Yet, Paul's clarity about his own behavior—which included a form of physical cruelty to innocent people—is sandwiched between a strong statement of his identity in Christ 'he judged me faithful, appointing me to his service' and the glory that God has received in saving him, that 'Jesus Christ might display his perfect patience as an example to those who were to believe in him for eternal life.' This understanding of his sin in relationship to his own identity in Christ and the glory of God leads him to unbridled worship: 'To the King of the ages, immortal, invisible, the only God, be honor and glory for ever and ever. Amen.' Likewise, our desire is that an abusive man seeing his sin in all its ugliness and taking the first steps toward Spirit-wrought change, would lead to praise of the King, not shame.

Consider asking him to rewrite Paul's testimony in 1 Timothy 1:12-17 in his own words, applying it to himself. For example, instead of 'he judged me faithful, appointing me to his service...', how would he state how Christ views him? And how has God been glorified in his story?

For accepting consequences and seeking amends, you should help him continually identify the effects of his sin. This sets him up to correct the wrong he has caused—not to clear his name or get others to capitulate, but rather with no expectations attached.

Deliverable: *The next step of development of the Inventory of Abusive Behaviors, is for each item on the list, to identify the harm done to the victim and what he will do to make it right.*

Identifying the harm done to the victim will mean listening to the pain she expresses, either directly to the abuser or indirectly through others.[13] But this deliverable is more than listening. He needs to put in his own words a description of what harmful effects his behaviors had on her. He should then also describe what actions he should take to make amends for each of the behaviors. The examples above may be a good primer as you guide him through this process.

Is He Establishing a Demonstrable TURN From His Abusive Patterns?

Repentance is a fruit of saving faith. And fruit takes a while to grow. Just as a fruit tree has the beginning expressions of fruit—green tips emerging as flower blossoms—that move to the fullest expression—fruit set emerging into fruit maturity—so repentance moves from seeing and owning to hating and turning. Actually turning from sin is the fullest expression of repentance.

In 2 Corinthians 7:10-11, Paul acknowledges healthy fruit in the lives of those in the church in Corinth whom he had previously rebuked. He notes the following specific fruit of repentance that shows him that they have godly, not worldly, grief: earnestness, eagerness to clear themselves, indignation (toward their sin), fear (of the Lord), longing, zeal, and punishment (willingness to accept consequences). This fruit is observable to Paul—even from a distance.[14] The theme of this

---

13. This is why input from the victim's counselor is vital to what happens with the abusive husband—particularly as that counselor has a deeper understanding of the traumatic aspects of the effects of abuse. It is worth really spending some time here to help the abuser understand the damage that is done.

14. It is important to remind ourselves that Paul was able to observe this fruit from a distance, because often people will make the argument: 'How can we tell if a spouse is repentant if the couple is still separated?' But we see from Paul's example here that it is possible to see good

list is consistent, observable change that is evident to those who shared Paul's original concerns.

Changed behaviors establish themselves over time. The more established a new pattern is, the greater the likelihood it is a lasting change. This statement is neither legalistic nor perfectionistic. While we recognize that no one is perfectly freed from sin's influence in this life and thus a man who is recovering from being abusive will never be completely free of sinful thoughts and urges, he nevertheless *can* be completely free of abusive behaviors that inflict harm on others.

Practical Strategy: At this point, the abusive spouse demonstrates motivation to change. The amends process has started the process of change by replacing destructive and unhealthy behaviors with righteous, healthy ones. Scripture is rich with imagery on such decisive replacement. The 'put off and put on' texts from Colossians 3 and Ephesians 4 are powerful motivation for thinking through the specifics of what 'old man' behaviors he needs to put off and what 'new man' behaviors he needs to put on. You can also make use of God's specific direction to husbands in Ephesians 5:25-32, Colossians 3:19, and 1 Peter 3:7 in formulating his agenda for change.

Deliverable: Based on the work he has put into the Inventory of Abusive Behaviors *tool, the husband can create an agenda for change that the church, the spouse, and the husband himself can agree upon (along with the counselors involved in the situation). Practically, it may work best to have the husband start a new section of the* Inventory *document labeled* Committed Changes, *which is made up of two simple sections: (1) Commitment to Heart Change, where he lists the specific beliefs and desires that will be different from before. (2)*

---

fruit even when you aren't in close contact with the abuser, or in close proximity to him.

Commitment to Behavior Change, where he lists the specific behaviors that will be different than before.

What Comes Next?

Genuine repentance will lead to the reconciliation of a man to his Lord, and this is the main goal in working with a former abuser. Genuine repentance will sometimes result in reconciliation with his spouse as well, and this is also a desirable outcome. We have emphasized throughout this book that marriage counseling is contra-indicated in the initial stages of counseling for domestic abuse, and we have encouraged you to remind the abuser that the goal is reconciliation of himself to the Lord, not reconciliation of the marriage.

But in some situations, reliable reconciliation becomes possible at the point of established repentance. We suggest the following guidelines when trying to determine when marriage counseling for the purpose of reconciliation is a safe and productive option.

- Marriage counseling is never appropriate as long as there are emotional or physical safety issues between the couple. You should not encourage couples to meet together when one of them feels unsafe in the presence of the other.

- Marriage counseling should not occur until the abuser can take responsibility for his abuse. Until that point, the abuser is very likely to try to manipulate the counselor or the counseling session in order to avoid responsibility or mutualize the responsibility for the abuse by pointing out the flaws in his partner.

- Generally, we recommend that a couple wait to initiate couples counseling or marriage reconciliation work until fruit of genuine repentance has been established for a few months, as verified by the team (shepherding/accountability team, victim and her counselor and/or advocate, abuser and his counselor).

- We also recommend that both parties understand a clear process whereby she can alert church leadership of any concerns she has for old patterns emerging. The former abuser should not only agree to, but welcome, this accountability.

- The *Committed Changes* section of the *Inventory of Abusive Behaviors* should function as a document of expectations for accountability and progress in the marriage.

We know that waiting this long to initiate couples counseling or doing marriage work often creates significant hardships for the family. But we contend that continuing or enabling the abuse is worse. Encourage couples who are recovering from a destructive relationship to invest the time in their individual work so that they are really ready to work on the marriage before they start couples counseling or marriage reconciliation programs in their church.

9

Leading Your Church to Respond With Wisdom and Compassion

Abusiveness has little to do with psychological problems and everything to do with values and beliefs. Where do a boy's values about partner relationships come from? The sources are many... In sum, a boy's values develop from the full range of his experiences within his *culture*.—Lundy Bancroft[1]

You know that those who are considered rulers of the Gentiles lord it over them, and their great ones exercise authority over them. But it shall not be so among you. But whoever would be great among you must be your servant, and whoever would be first among you must be slave of all (Mark 10:42-44).

---

1. Lundy Bancroft, *Why Does He Do That? Inside the Minds of Angry and Controlling Men* (New York: Berkley Books, 2002), 319.

Abuse sends shockwaves through the community. At least, it ought to. It ought to disturb the people of God. Earlier we made the case that God made the church to be the Spirit-indwelled people of the Word who are together learning to love what God loves and to hate what God hates. The beliefs and values conveyed in the pages of Scripture find their embodiment in living people. Jesus wanted the church to be the one type of community in all the world that demonstrates authority as self-emptying service for the good of those under it. In the church, greatness is demonstrated in servanthood (Matt. 20:25-28). When abuse is foreign and outrageous to God's people, the church is reinforcing God's perspective.

In this chapter, we want to help you think short term and long term about how to shepherd your entire congregation on this painful topic. In the short term, we want to help you communicate wisely to your church about the present situation you're walking through. For the long term, we want to help you establish a culture of moral clarity regarding abuse.

Communicating About the Present Situation

When abuse occurs in your church, the effects are not just relegated to the abusive home. Guiding the community of faith to respond rightly is another difficult part of shepherding well in tragic situations like this.

In this section, we will suggest a strategy for shepherding your congregation about how to think about and respond to the present situation. This is not merely a communication strategy to help you effectively convey your message or to do damage control. No, this is a strategy to help your people grow in their love for hurting people—specifically, to offer supportive care to victims and discerning care to abusers. Church leaders call

God's people to act with humility, compassion, and courage in these situations.

The form of communication may be different for each church. In large churches, this communication may only happen within their house church, small group, or Sunday School class. In much smaller churches, it might occur in a member meeting of the whole church. But we advise you to communicate about the situation with the highest level of discretion and only bring in the parties who need to know. Consistent with what we have shared earlier, any communication about the abuse should only occur with the express advice and consent of the victim. Electronic or written communication is not advisable. We suggest face-to-face conversation with committed members of the church who know the parties involved that includes the following components.[2]

Opening Summary

We have become aware of a concerning situation in the home of some members of this community. This is a painful situation, but we are grateful it has come to the light so that we can offer pastoral care and guidance. We want our church community to know that we are committed to responding (1) with the right heart, (2) with the right process, and (3) as the right kind of church community. We will explain each of these components of our response. But first, let us give an overview of the situation. This overview may be difficult for some of you to hear, particularly if you have suffered abuse in the past. We

---

2. We advise consulting with a lawyer when addressing the personal situations publicly. Ideally, you want one who understands the tension of value between the legal consideration of mitigating liability and the ecclesiological consideration of holding members of the congregation accountable.

want you to know that your pastors want to help you if that's the case.

The purpose of an opening summary is to give a global view of what church members are about to hear. A statement like this prepares them for difficult news, while making it clear that there is an established plan of response. This statement also commends the victim for disclosing what was occurring behind closed doors, which will go a long way in establishing the community value of safety for those who need protection.

Overview of the Situation

Once you've oriented people to what they're about to hear, you should give them a general description of the situation. In this description, you want to avoid details that will unnecessarily expose the victim to public scrutiny or give leverage to the abuser if he wants to build a public case against her or against the process the church has taken in addressing him. Stick to the basic facts of the situation that have become apparent in the process thus far. Be careful not to over-explain your reasons for seeing the situation the way you are seeing it—too much focus on justifying your conclusions will not serve the victim well, or the congregation for that matter. Instead, keep it straightforward. Also, prior to the meeting, you should run this overview by both the victim (for permission) and the abuser (less for permission and more out of respect to him).

The concerning situation involves the Jones family. Michelle shared with a friend that in their home Larry is harsh, hateful, and threatening toward her. That friend asked Michelle's permission to share this with Pastor David about six weeks ago. Both ladies did the right thing. It allowed us to listen to Michelle's concerns and approach Larry in the appropriate way.

A number of pastors and members of the congregation have been involved in offering care to Michelle and in establishing accountability for Larry. We are speaking of this publicly for two reasons: First, enough of our church is aware of the situation that we want to lead us to respond in a biblical and unified way. Second, the Joneses are presently separated because of the seriousness of the issue, and we want you to be assured of our awareness and continuing work with both Michelle and with Larry.

This example description attempts to give the basics of: who is involved, how church leadership became aware of it, why coming forward was the right thing to do, what the initial response was, and why this is still a developing situation.

You may have noticed the feature terms in that summary did not include *abuse*, but rather characteristics of *harsh*, *hateful*, and *threatening*. This is not because we think the word *abuse* should necessarily be avoided. Rather, it is a teaching strategy. Harshness, hatefulness and threats are biblical terminology for the character and tactics of abuse (Col. 3:19; Eph. 4:29; 6:9). Starting with biblical language helps your people understand God's concern for this and will help avoid triggering any prejudices that keep people from focusing on the actual urgency of the problem. Remember, people will have varying degrees of understanding regarding abuse, and some will have a visceral response of skepticism or defensiveness. If you start with biblical language in your summary, you at least increase the possibility of understanding when you describe abuse in the next part of the conversation.

(1) *We are committed to responding with the right heart.*

Once your congregation has been briefed on the general summary, you want to express the heart behind your response. By *heart*, we mean the biblical beliefs and values that shape your approach. We covered this more extensively in Chapter 2, so it may be helpful to review those ideas as you prepare for this conversation. But let us share some suggested values to feature publicly.

Responding with hearts that are like God's means being guided by the right truths and committed to the right values. Here are a few of the main commitments guiding our approach:

• **God designed the home to be a place where His character is displayed. What occurs in the home is not merely a private matter, but a matter of discipleship for the church.**
When Scripture addresses the family, it does so in the context of the larger community of faith (Deut. 6:4-9; Col. 3:18-25). In God's design of the Church, families are not independent, self-contained kingdoms. Each member of a family is accountable to the broader community of God's people. What happens in the home, then, is of great importance to the Church. Walking openly in community, in fact, is one of the greatest spiritual protections God put in place for His people (Eph. 4:15-16; 1 John 1:5-10). This is especially important when we consider those in the Church who are more likely to find themselves in vulnerable situations, like being dependent on someone who'd prefer to keep things in the dark.

- *A particularly difficult problem to bring to the light is abuse, and it's our duty as shepherds of this church to take it seriously when it does.*

Abuse is difficult to bring to the light for a number of reasons, but let's feature two of them: It often feels shameful to disclose and difficult to identify.

A wife experiencing harsh treatment from her husband will often feel confused and embarrassed, uncertain of how she should think about what is happening to her. Often, it's easier not to say anything, hoping she can just manage the situation as best she can.

But it's also difficult to identify when harshness should be considered abusive. Maybe hearing the word abuse even right now feels unclear. But now is not the time to define all these things. We simply want to acknowledge that abuse is a difficult issue to understand, especially for those who by God's grace have not been exposed to it. We also want to assure you of our commitment to think biblically about it.

- *When any measure of abuse occurs in a marriage, the problem is not with the marriage but with the person who is acting abusively.*

Abuse is not primarily about how two people relate to one another. It's about how one person sees the world—how he views himself, his wife, and ultimately God. We will of course pay pastoral attention to the whole marriage and weigh all of the concerns appropriately. But in any complex situation with a variety of concerns, responding wisely requires you to prioritize those concerns. Protecting anyone who is vulnerable to harm gets priority.

Here is another way to think about why we believe it is in keeping with God's heart to prioritize the concerns this way: Husbands are uniquely responsible to lead with the gentleness and selflessness of the Lord Jesus Christ. That means the abuse of authority is particularly offensive to God because it lies about who He is and harms people He loves.

In God's design of the family, a husband leads in reflecting God's character—displaying the sacrificial love of Christ in the way he leads his wife (Eph 5:25-33). The onus of leading is uniquely on him, and thus the onus of responsibility is also on him. Those who are given authority are held to stricter account than those who are given less (Mark 9:42-50; 10:42-45; James 3:1). So, when a husband uses his authority not according to God's design, but to serve himself and harm others, it has particularly significant consequences. In other words, with authority comes greater responsibility and accountability.

• **The transformative power of the gospel of Jesus Christ is the only ultimate solution to the problem of abuse. The gospel will guide the entire process of our church's response.** *Abuse is not just outward actions, but an inward attitude of the heart. As we have taught countless times at this church, the most fundamental problem with us as people is the sinfulness that resides in our own hearts (Matt. 15:16-20). The problem is so profound, that no strategy or therapy we can come up with can solve it.*

With man this is impossible, but with God all things are possible (Matt. 19:26). The Bible says that the grace of God brings salvation from the penalty of the sins we've committed and it trains us to no longer be dominated by the heart desires that led to it (Titus 2:11). When a man is transformed by the gospel, it is not just words admitting wrong, but a transformed life that demonstrates itself over time in changed behaviors and words. The discipline of the Lord is painful, but it later yields the peaceful fruit of righteousness to those who have been trained by it (Heb. 12:11). Our commitment is to present the gospel and watch carefully for its fruits.

That is the heart behind our response. But we also want you to be aware of the process this heart commitments lead to.

(2) We are committed to responding with the right process.

The right heart leads to the right action. We have arranged a process of care that seeks to prioritize what we believe are God's priorities in this situation.

• **We have received Michelle's disclosure of abuse and have a safety plan to protect her. We will continue to care for and advise her.**
Michelle did the right thing in coming forward, and we received her concerns with what we hope is compassion and wisdom. We believe no one should passively subject themselves to ongoing abuse. The Lord did not design marriage to be abusive; nor did He design the church to be passive when abuse is discovered. We have a plan in place that will not allow abusive interactions to continue without consequence.

We are caring for Michelle as a church with counsel and practical support. We are also involving community resources when appropriate. In it all, we are encouraging her to trust in the Lord.

• **We have sought to address Larry with this accusation of abuse in order to bring accountability to him.**
When approaching a situation like this, you have to recognize that the common wisdom that there are two sides to every story cannot be the only guiding principle. You also have to recognize the principle that the deeds of darkness like to stay in the dark.

In other words, a person doesn't see their own sin as clearly as someone with fresh eyes and a biblical mindset.

We're caring for Larry by putting fresh eyes on his home and bringing a biblical mindset to the patterns of interaction he's established. We are helping him understand God's perspective of his home and holding him to biblical standards of accountability and repentance. As we know from Scripture, sanctification is often a long and difficult process. In this case, it will take a lot of direct involvement from others over time. We are seeking to put the right people around Larry to help him.

• **We will seek to offer biblically sound counsel about the marriage based on careful consideration of the vital factors at play.**

The implications on the marriage will become clear in the long term. But be assured that your pastors will seek to give biblically sound counsel that both honors God's beautiful design of marriage and takes seriously the factors at play in individual marriages in a fallen world, as both Jesus and Paul do in Scripture.

As you're first hearing about this situation, a question that may have jumped immediately to mind is what will happen with the marriage. This may be the most tempting issue to discuss among yourselves. You serve everyone best by refraining from speculation and instead praying for them.

In fact, this admonition is a natural segue to our last commitment.

(3) We are committed to responding as the right kind of church community.

We must be a community characterized by the heart of God in how we collectively respond to this situation.

- *We will not gossip or speculate. We will share knowledge with those who can actually do good in the situation.*

As a community of Christians called to love one another, we must resist the temptation to speculate or to have an I-knew-something-was-wrong kind of attitude. Conversations like that do not accomplish anything other than tickling our own ears, including both personal conversations and social media posts. But we have a hurting family in our midst, and we need to be extra careful to protect them from what Scripture calls the 'strife of tongues' (Ps. 31:20).

If you have knowledge or experience of a situation that would be important to know, please share it with someone who can actually use it to benefit the situation. Share it with pastors or appointed members who you know are helping in the situation. Don't share it with people not involved in the care of this family.

- *We will not divide ourselves into 'sides,' but rather ask what role we can play in helping. For most in the church, it will be to pray.*

These situations can quickly devolve into who takes what side. We are asking that you guard your hearts against this. The main way to avoid this is to do what we just said—avoid gossip and speculation. Some of you may feel particularly close to one spouse or the other. Let that motivate you to pray and to express personal support, certainly.

But remember the best way to support this family is to contribute to a unified plan of care and accountability. Our first loyalty should always be to Christ's purposes in a person's like. You can be assured that church leadership is seeking this purpose, even if that means personal discomfort for those involved.

- *We will take stock of our own hearts before the Lord regarding how we treat one another in our own homes.* Painful situations like this show us how disruptive and harmful sin in the home is. We are wise to take warning ourselves. The Bible describes sin not as someone else's problem, but as a propensity of every human heart. Christians are responsible to place priority on taking stock of their own sin before identifying it in others (Matt. 7:1-5). Jesus told His followers to beware and be watchful of the dangers within each one of them.

The home is sacred not because family relationships are our highest loyalty, but because family relationships are where we foremost display our highest loyalty to the Lord Jesus Christ, to love those He's called us to love in the way He's called us to love them. We want to be a church that joyfully obeys God in our homes.

Thank you for letting us speak to you on this difficult matter. May the Lord give us strength to respond in ways that bring honor to His name. Please pray for everyone involved in this situation, and for Michelle in particular. She's really hurting right now.

A Culture of Moral Clarity Regarding Abuse

In this last section, we want to leave you with a positive vision of the right kind of culture to work for in your church. Unlike the previous section, this one contains no specific strategy. Instead, it is meant to suggest some principles to promote in the regular course of your public ministries. This section, then, is less about responding to a specific situation in your church and more about creating the right kind of atmosphere beforehand. Our intent is to offer principles that you can proactively promote to encourage the kind of church culture where abuse cannot easily hide.

We offer the following ideas to integrate into your preaching, teaching, and public prayer gatherings as is fitting. This list is not intended to hijack the regular teaching ministry of the church, which we believe should be comprised of expository preaching and Bible-centered teaching. Rather, they are ideas to be aware of as you apply Scripture to the pressing issues your people face. One of those issues, sadly, is abuse in the home, whether in their own lives, the lives of those they love, or the lives of those they are witnessing to.

We start with general ideas and move to ideas more specifically related to abuse.

- *As you affirm submission to authority as a biblical value, make sure you warn against the abuse of authority as well.* Churches trying to promote a biblical understanding of God and of human relationships will recognize the legitimacy of authority, and defend it against an anti-authority culture. But to do full justice to the Bible's teaching on authority, we must recognize the many warnings against its misuse. If we fail to do this, people will believe that passive submission to any authority is what God calls them to do. This reinforces an atmosphere where abuse can grow.

- *As you affirm and teach a biblical theology of suffering, make sure that you also affirm a biblical theology of oppression.* We have discussed this in Chapter 2 under the heading 'Abuse is a Form of Oppression' and in footnote 7. Church leaders often provide care that is reckless and counsel that is harmful when they do not affirm that God hates oppression in all its forms, that God hears the cries of the oppressed and delivers them, and that God's people are called to respond to oppression by caring for the oppressed and correcting the oppressor.

- *As you affirm the unique roles of a husband and a wife, make sure you warn against the dangerous misuse of those roles.* For all of us, biblical ideas get mixed in with cultural preferences in how we see important issues, including our perception of male and female roles. Church leaders rightly warn against the flattening of unique roles God made beautiful—a husband is the head of his wife, and a wife is the confidence of her husband. But you must also warn against an ungodly version of headship that considers men superior to women and disparages their essential contribution to the family, the church, and the world.

- *As you speak about the priorities of Christian manhood, publicly call men to show concern for the safety of the vulnerable among them.* Jesus was the paradigm of a man, and His disciples were constantly surprised by Jesus' concern for people they considered unimportant (like women and children) or unclean (like prostitutes and lepers). Jesus' ambitions did not fit the standard ambitions of His day, and neither should ours. As you teach men in your church about priorities, do not speak merely of personal success in the Christian life. Charge them to use their strength to care for those without it.

- *When you address sin in your public teaching, do not focus only on the sins you see out in the world, but on sins that may be tripping your own people up.* Self-righteousness is spring-loaded in the soul, and sometimes preachers and teachers can promote self-righteousness by declaring the ugliness of sins they see in the world. These warnings are necessary and good. But without a balanced diet that also addresses sins more likely to characterize your own church, you will dull people's awareness of their need for grace themselves.

- *As you talk to your people about sin, be sure to describe it not merely as external action but as inward disposition.*

A healthy awareness of personal sin is essential to a lifestyle of repentance. It is easier to speak publicly about the external behaviors of sin—yelling, insulting, threatening. But harder to help people understand the anger inside of them that leads to it. Make the effort to describe how sin operates in the heart, urging us to take hold of our desires through any means necessary.

- *As you speak of the Christian life, give due respect to the power of weakness.* A healthy awareness of personal need is also essential to the Christian life. As much as we'd like to convince ourselves otherwise, all of us have problems we cannot solve on our own. As we see in the apostle Paul's life, awareness of his own weakness was the necessary condition for the power of God to be displayed. We must not set our people up for failure by helping them coddle the illusion of their own strength.

- *More specifically now, make your church aware that abuse is a present danger.* Address this as a problem in our culture that Jesus Christ alone has the ultimate answer to. Just like Christians are rightly alarmed by legal abortion or racial injustice, they ought to be alarmed by the prevalence of domestic abuse in our society. But also cross the threshold of your own church doors as you discuss abuse. Acknowledge that it may even be troubling families in your own congregation. This will help create a culture of awareness and receptivity on this issue.

- *Publicly assure women that specific disclosures of abuse will be wisely received.* The fear of not being believed is one of the strongest reasons a person who is being victimized by abuse doesn't come forward. Church leaders can help undermine this fear by communicating proactively. It shows both awareness of their plight and receptivity to their concern. Such a public assurance will not guarantee they come forward when they need to, but it certainly undermines a significant roadblock. Some churches post signs in the women's restroom stating that abuse is an abhorrent desecration of the image of God, that it will be taken seriously and treated discreetly by church leaders, and provide a name and contact information for the staff member or church leader who will receive confidential reports. Other churches have a domestic abuse policy, similar to the child protection policies that almost all churches have. We have included a sample domestic abuse policy in Appendix D. Making this policy public to your members will encourage victims to come forward and will hold the church accountable to care for them and to correct abusers in the ways that we have outlined in this book.

Conclusion

We want to end how we began: with some encouragement to you.

Remember, you are an agent of a love much bigger than you. God's love goes beyond sentiment, actually accomplishing good in someone else's life. By working through this book, you have shown dedication to the interests of someone who needs an advocate. You are displaying God's disposition toward hurting people. This should encourage you greatly. The love required to bring healing in this situation does not come from you. You are just an agent of God's love. So love the one who is hurting and has been for a long time. God will give you strength.

This book has been an imperfect attempt to help you take wise action. And your attempt to take wise action will also be imperfect. But take heart. The Lord delights in using imperfect people to accomplish His perfect will. Your confidence is not in yourself, but in the Savior who comes to redeem sinners from their sin and to bring justice to the oppression of sin. We know this because Jesus Christ, through the prophet Isaiah, says this about Himself.

The Spirit of the Lord GOD is upon me,
    because the LORD has anointed me
to bring good news to the poor;
    he has sent me to bind up the brokenhearted,
to proclaim liberty to the captives,
    and the opening of the prison to those who are bound;
to proclaim the year of the LORD's favor,
    and the day of vengeance of our God;
    to comfort all who mourn;
to grant to those who mourn in Zion—
    to give them a beautiful headdress instead of ashes,
the oil of gladness instead of mourning,
    the garment of praise instead of a faint spirit;
that they may be called oaks of righteousness,
    the planting of the LORD, that he may be glorified.
(Isa. 61:1-3)

Appendix A:

FAQs on Domestic Abuse Care

What if I think a wife is falsely accusing her husband?
Your first task is not to attempt to discern the reliability of the claim of abuse; rather, your first task is to care for the safety of the person claiming abuse. Much like in the fog of war you can't know every factor at play in a threatening situation, so in an abuse disclosure you can't know everything you need to at first. So, you take immediate action based on guiding priorities. That priority is the safety of any potential victim, regardless of your first impression.

Let's unpack that. False accusations of abuse are far less frequent than abusive situations. Your initial reaction to hearing an accusation may be tuned to the opposite assumption. You may, hopefully, be personally unfamiliar with the experience of abuse. On top of this, you may really love and respect the person being accused. But these good things can gear your gut instincts wrongly.

Your immediate sense of a situation is the expression of a limited perspective—the associations you make based off of your own limited experience. What makes you believe one type of person over another might be exactly wrong. Your gauge may be off when it comes to recognizing the subtle dynamics at play.

So what should we rely on in guarding against false claims? Not your own instincts, but a carefully laid out process that's based on the right principles and that prioritizes the right values. The leading value is to represent the Lord's concern for potential harm being done to vulnerable people. As the process unfolds from that value, a clearer picture of what is occurring in the home will emerge. You should also rely on the team that you have put in place, including people (advocates/counselors) with training and experience in domestic abuse.

Once you have a safety plan established, you can help a potential victim process her experience from the framework of abuse laid out in this book. This will help you together gain clarity on whether the essential indicators of abuse are present, as outlined in earlier chapters.

At this point, sometimes a potential victim will herself conclude that the concerning behavior does not constitute abuse. In this case, indicate that as you address on her behalf the sinful patterns that are nevertheless present in the marriage, you wish to remain vigilant over any potential indicators of abuse. In most of the situations we have seen in which this question has been raised, *something* concerning is going on. It may not be enough to be considered abusive, but it is nevertheless a significant concern.

Even if what emerges does not fit the description of abuse we've laid out here, something deeply concerning is going on in the home that will require pastoral courage to press into.

It will take time and effort. It may take counseling expertise beyond what you can offer. But it must not be left unaddressed. This is why staying committed to a process that brings clarity is so important. The ultimate goal is not merely to determine whether we call it abuse or not, but rather to understand the particular dynamics of *this* home, and respond wisely to whatever is going on.

If this careful process, which prioritized the safety of any potential victims and ideally involved consulting with counselors or victim advocates familiar with abuse dynamics, reveals a wrongful accusation, then explore *why* the spouse made this claim. The *why* may be for reasons that could be considered *weakness* and in need of patient care or for reasons that could be considered *intentional* and in need of correction. Often it's a mix of both.

In cases of *weakness*, the reason for accusation could be anything from a misunderstanding of what constitutes abuse to a broader pattern of fear in the spouse's life. Be compassionate in your guidance, assuring her of your ongoing vigilance. In cases of *intentionality*, the reason for accusation could be anything from deep dissatisfaction with her marriage to an attempt to justify leaving her spouse, often for another relationship. Appeal to her by helping her recognize what desires are driving this behavior, and show how those desires line up with what Scripture says leads to life.

What should I do if people at my church think she's falsely accusing her husband?

Speaking publicly about your willingness to receive victims may cause some fear among some about the possibility of false accusations. This fear is understandable, and should be publicly acknowledged. But this fear can be assuaged by the *process* of receiving victims. Receiving concerns is not simple or reactionary. It is not a virtue crusade or a witch hunt.

Rather, it means that a victim is taken at her word rather than dismissed, is made aware of the resources available to her rather than left alone, and is given a clear plan forward rather than accepting the status quo. If a false accusation has occurred, the process will eventually reveal that fact. But the possibility of false accusation is a risk worth taking for the greater value of protecting the vulnerable.

As a church leader, you must guard your own heart from making decisions based on the fear of being misunderstood or criticized for laying out a process that values the safety of any potential victim. To put it frankly, you cannot be scared of being criticized for supporting a woman some people may have dismissed as crazy.

As you lead in a difficult situation like this, do not respond to people's questions by emphasizing which spouse you 'side' with, but rather by emphasizing the principles that guided your response to a difficult situation: for instance, the safety of anyone who is vulnerable, the distinction between non-abusive and abusive sin, the reality that sin likes to hide, and humility as an indicator of genuine repentance.

It's an unfortunate tendency of human nature that people will establish their opinions without adequate information, based on any number of personal associations and preferences. Many people at church cannot imagine abuse dynamics or may even have a low opinion of the woman prior. This will influence the way they process the limited information they pick up.

What if, even though I'm concerned a husband is acting abusively, I think the wife is also acting manipulatively, or otherwise sinfully?

A wife may very well be acting sinfully in the situation, for a variety of reasons. This should in no way alter your commitment to her safety. Whatever sin she may be practicing does not pose the same threat as the abuse she is suffering. As a church leader, you must still take her concerns seriously and in good faith, and follow practices that value the safety of victims.

In the course of making provisions for her safety and walking her through how to think about her situation, you will eventually address how she can think biblically and respond faithfully to her suffering. This task takes great care to avoid implying blame on the victim for the abusive behaviors of her abuser. No level of sinfulness on her part warrants another person to act abusively. Assure her often of this fact, even as you help her see how her own sinful response is not God's will in human relationships, and will therefore never result in greater peace and security. For both God's glory and her own good, appeal to her to act with wisdom, courage, and love to others in her suffering.

The best person to confront sin or manipulation in a person is someone with a close relationship who has earned the right to have hard conversations with her. This could be her advocate, or her counselor, or a close friend. The best way to address sinful behaviors in a situation like this is not through direct correction at first, but rather through helping her to identify the desires behind those behaviors. You may discover along with her that her desire for security or affirmation are behind her sin. Help her understand God's heart toward her regarding such desires, showing where manipulation is at least in part a failure to trust that heart. Often, a hurting person feels the need to defend her self-interest because she's lived so long with those who haven't acted for her good.

You may also uncover patterns of sin or manipulation that preceded her marriage and the abuse that occurred in it. You love her by addressing this only in the right time and situation. Only after her safety has been established will it be fruitful to address any patterns of manipulation or sinful response on her part. To address these before this will strongly imply that her wrong responses caused the abuse. But we also want to note that failing to address her manipulative responses in the long-term counseling process, perhaps out of a misguided understanding of compassion, will not lead to long-term peace for her or glory to God. You must treat her with the dignity of being made in God's image, and thus responsible for her own responses to her suffering. Her fate is not determined by what happened to her, but by the Holy Spirit's power in her to overcome.

What do I do when the situation before me doesn't seem to fit the description of abuse in this book?

If you're asking this question, you are likely facing a care situation in which abuse is being described, but what you see doesn't seem to square with what we described in Section 1. Perhaps you wonder if 'abuse' is the right word for what you are seeing. Perhaps you don't see, or the spouse you're caring for doesn't report, the kind of diminished personhood that we described in Chapter 2. Perhaps you see what we described in Chapter 3 as 'competitor' sins ('me before you'), rather than 'predator/parasite' sins ('me over you'). This is a good question.

First, we want to remind you that it is not your job to be a forensic investigator. Hopefully this comes as a relief to you. Unless you have special training in mental health care, domestic abuse intervention, social work, or some other relevant, specialized field, please take that burden off of yourself. You do not have to bear it. Actually, even if you do have that kind of specialized training, you probably shouldn't be applying it to a complex situation with a couple with whom you enjoy a close relationship. Better to let other eyes that have a little more objectivity take a look at the situation. We have provided an extensive list of resources in Appendix D that can be really helpful. We want to emphasize that this is not something you have to figure out on your own.

Second, it is possible that the relationship in front of you is what our friend Leslie Vernick refers to as a 'difficult' or 'disappointing' relationship, rather than a destructive one.[1] Her work can shed some helpful light on that topic. Another friend, Darby Strickland, has written an entire book on the topic of identifying domestic abuse—appropriately named, *Is It Abuse?*[2] Darby's book devotes entire chapters to each of the primary categories of abuse: physical, sexual, emotional, spiritual, and financial. These alternative resources may help you as you help your friend, family member, or church member better understand what is going on in her marriage.

One last important word of reminder: unless you are living in the home yourself, you cannot possibly be a better judge of what is happening inside the home than those who live there. And if one or more of those people is telling you that they are being hurt within their home, you have an obligation to take them seriously and care for them accordingly.

As we said in response to an earlier question, even if you conclude that the concerns in the marriage do not fit the description of abuse we've laid out here, something deeply concerning may be going on in the home that will require pastoral courage to press into. It will take time and effort. It may take counseling expertise beyond what you can offer. But it must not be left unaddressed. This is why staying committed to a process that brings clarity is so important. The ultimate goal is not merely to determine whether we call it abuse or not, but rather to understand the particular dynamics of *this* home, and respond wisely to whatever is going on. We pray that the

---

1. Leslie Vernick, 'Are You in an Emotionally Destructive Marriage?', Chapter 1 of *The Emotionally Destructive Marriage: How to Find Your Voice and Reclaim Your Hope*, 7-27.

2. Darby A. Strickland, *Is It Abuse?: A Biblical Guide to Identifying Domestic Abuse and Helping Victims* (Phillipsburg, NJ: P&R Publishing, 2020).

foregoing chapters serve as a help to you as you seek, with the Spirit's help, to care wisely in a hard and uncertain situation.

How should our approach to care change if we think that the abuser may have another condition which may be contributing to his behavior?

There is some overlap between some of the factors that contribute to domestic abuse and the symptoms of Autism Spectrum Disorder (ASD), Attention Deficit Disorder (ADD/ADHD), Obsessive Compulsive Disorder (OCD), mood disorders, some of the personality disorders, and other disorders. Obviously, if anyone is exhibiting symptoms of some of these conditions, they should see a professional mental health provider for diagnosis and treatment. Diagnosis of a comorbid condition can certainly help explain, and treatment can sometimes help reduce, some of the abusive behavior.

If he is still being abusive, everything we said in the earlier chapters about caring for victims and correcting abusers is still true. The existence of the co-occurring condition is not an excuse for abusive behavior. If he wants to eliminate or reduce his abusive behavior, the abusive individual must be willing to pursue treatment for his co-occurring condition, as well as for his abusive behavior. Generally speaking, these treatments can usually proceed along somewhat parallel tracks—although sometimes finances or the requirements of a specific treatment may prohibit simultaneous treatment.

Appendix B:

FAQs on Separation, Divorce, and Reunification After Abuse

The most difficult decisions in human life are those that present us with values in tension with one another. Good, biblical values like marriage, forgiveness and reconciliation can be in tension with other good, biblical values like accountability, protection, and justice.

This tension becomes more pronounced in more extreme situations such as domestic or sexual abuse, where the factors involved are:

- Difficult to discern. In other words, the factors at play are not readily apparent, but have dynamics that are hidden—often intentionally—from plain sight.

- Have greater potential of harm. In other words, the factors at play could do some serious damage to vulnerable people (both acute short term and gradual long term).

- Various/Numerous. In other words, the significant factors that need to be investigated, addressed, and ongoingly evaluated are too abundant to do in a short amount of time.

This requires a response that is diligent to accumulate the factors necessary for responsible action in unclear, threatening situations. When considering reunification, the greater the degree of difficulty to discern, potential for harm, and variety of issues, the greater

- the amount of time needs to be.
- the number of viewpoints needs to be.
- the knowledge of common abuse dynamics needs to be.
- the knowledge of the specific dynamics in this family needs to be.
- the biblical understanding of how to assess these dynamics needs to be.

The purpose of this appendix is to help with the last of these needs, since Scripture is the framework from which we evaluate the other factors.

Biblical Values in Tension

Scripture never contradicts itself, since it is inspired by the same all-wise, unchanging God from Genesis through Revelation. However, Scripture does not present a view of the world that is one dimensional and simplistic. Scripture recognizes tension in a fallen world.

Instead of providing a simple index of the exact right response to any situation we find ourselves in, Scripture provides guiding principles that we then, in reliance on the Holy Spirit, use to discern how best to respond to our situation. This is a dynamic process that requires us to acknowledge multiple biblical angles from which to consider our lives.

The following chart is intended to set biblical principles in proper tension with one another, which will allow you to think about the present situation you're helping with.

Biblical Principles Showing Potential Value of Reunification	Biblical Principles Showing Potential Dangers of Reunification
Marriage is a union designed by God, sealed by a covenant between husband and wife. God designed marriage as a permanent relationship, not as a temporary, customizable relationship that rises and falls on personal preferences. It is a union that should not be abandoned once it has been established. (Gen. 2:24; Mark 10:7-9)	Marriage is permanent not ontologically (as if the *being* of two spouses is somehow permanently bound), but rather in terms of its design purpose, as described on the left. God-given exceptions for divorce show that the union of two spouses can be separated in God's estimation because a covenant can be broken, even between people and God. Scripture contains no notion of God continuing in a covenant with covenant-breaking people (Jer. 3:1-10), but instead makes a new covenant where He transforms His people into covenant-keepers (Jer. 31:31-34). God arranges our salvation by arranging both parties as covenant-keepers. When the marriage covenant is abandoned by covenant-breaking sins, the innocent party is not obligated to sustain an illusion of union (Matt. 5:32; 19:9; 22:30, 1 Cor. 7:15).

Forgiveness is commanded in Scripture for all Christians as a sign that they have themselves been forgiven. When God shows His mercy to a sinner, that sinner shows mercy to others, even at great cost to him- or herself. (Matt. 18:21-35; Eph. 4:32)	Scripture talks about forgiveness dimensionally, not flatly. Forgiveness is displayed (1) as an internal willingness to forgive (Mark 11:25-26) but also (2) as an external relational exchange that requires a person to acknowledge their wrong according to God's standards (Matt. 18:15-20). Where there is not acknowledgment (saying the same thing as God does about sin), forgiveness cannot be granted (1 John 1:8-10). Discerning whether someone has come to agree with God about their sin requires a process commensurate with the degree of their deception.
Scripture links forgiveness with reconciliation, both to God and to people. One of the great hopes in human relationships is that someone can be received even after they have sinned. (2 Cor. 5:18-21; Eph. 2:16; Matt. 18:15-20)	Forgiveness and reconciliation are contingent on repentance. Repentance can only be responsibly discerned as a long-term pattern, particularly when others' safety is at stake (2 Cor. 7:10-12). The estrangement that comes as part of sin's curse will not be entirely reversed until the coming of the Lord. Extra care must be made to recognize the danger of false reconciliation when people are more vulnerable (Gen. 3; 2 Pet. 2:4-10). Love for God's people means protecting them from spiritual harm. If a person has a track record of harm, he must be handled differently (2 Tim. 2:16-18; Titus 3:10).

Love involves doing good to others at cost to self. It involves the sacrifice of preferring others' interests to one's own (John 15:13; Phil. 2:1-8).

Love bears all things, believes all things, hopes all things, endures all things (1 Cor. 13:7).

Love is doing good to another, and good is determined by righteousness. Sometimes love appears harsh, for the purpose of forcing recognition that unrighteousness is still present. To allow someone to perpetuate a lie is unloving, because it does not place him in the best place to see the truth: that their unrighteousness is separating them from God (Rom. 12:9; 1 Cor. 5:5; Heb. 12:11).

Love does not equal trust. No command is ever given in Scripture for one person to trust another person. Trust can be *un*loving if a person has demonstrated himself to be untrustworthy. Trusting him perpetuates his illusion. But God speaks about the dynamic of sin as a 'handing over' that takes a miracle of providence to reverse (Rom. 1:24, 26, 28).

God is honored when a wife trusts Him even when a husband refuses to obey the Word. When a wife is characterized by a gentle and quiet spirit instead of a manipulative one, she is being pleasing to the Lord. She therefore does not need to fear what would otherwise be frightening (1 Pet. 3:1-6).

Peter's instruction to wives in 1 Peter 3:1-6 is given in the context of Christians suffering injustice. In other words, Peter is recognizing their more vulnerable position. He is addressing their ability to influence their husbands—*not* with the manipulation of attraction, but rather with respectful and pure conduct. That's the main reasoning in the passage. There is no notion here that a quiet spirit means submission to abuse, since that would contradict the design purpose of marriage.

Furthermore, with the structure of this passage recognizing the unique vulnerability of women in marriages, Peter commands

	husbands to live with their wives by understanding the authority of God, the vulnerable position of his wife, and the stricter standards their influential position is held to (1 Pet. 3:7).

How do I tell if a husband who has been acting abusively is genuinely repentant?

Ultimately, you can't. But here's an indicator that might prove helpful as a gauge: new patterns of selfless behavior established over time in a context he no longer attempts to control. To put that more plainly, he establishes a new history of behavior free of both abuse *and* attempts to control access to his home. This is what humility looks like in a former abuser.

Let's unpack that. Only God ultimately knows the genuineness of a person's repentance. However, Christians are commanded to make great efforts to discern the reliability of a person's claim before validating him in community (Matt. 18:15-20; 2 Cor. 13:5-10, 7:10-13; 1 John 3:23-4:6). This is all the more urgent the more a person will have influence over others (Mark 9:42; James 3:1).

When you first address the spouse being accused of abuse, his response will likely be mixed. But his ongoing responses will eventually settle into a discernable pattern in one of two main directions: pride or humility.

Pride is displayed in an ongoing *unwillingness* to be questioned regarding his conduct, to allow corrective access to his home life, and to change behaviors that have adverse effects on his spouse. Such insistence on his own way usually confirms the accusation that abuse dynamics are present in the home, even if he denies it.

Humility is displayed in an ongoing *willingness* to be questioned regarding his conduct, to allow corrective access to his home life, and to change behaviors that have adverse effects on his spouse. Submission when he doesn't get his own way can indicate that the dynamics of the home are not abusive, though they may still be concerning.

What do I do if a husband is trying to repent from being abusive, but the wife won't forgive him and trust him?

Forgiveness and trust are not the same act. Both are a process, sure, but those processes are only related, not identical.

With forgiveness, we must distinguish between the *willingness* to forgive and the *granting* of forgiveness. Being *willing* to forgive is a universal command to all Christians, for they themselves have been forgiven (Matt. 18:21-35; Luke 6:37-38; Eph. 4:32). For someone who has been harmed, often in extremely cruel ways over years, to be willing to forgive the one who harmed her requires a miracle of grace. But to expect a victim to *grant* forgiveness without the abuser recognizing the harm done and requesting forgiveness is both unbiblical and cruel. The presumption of the granting of forgiveness throughout the Bible—both God-to-person and person-to-person—is confession of sin (Matt. 18:15-20; Luke 17:4; 2 Cor. 7:9-12). God grants forgiveness to anyone who repents, but He does not grant it to those who lighten, rationalize, or shift blame about their sin.

This question was specifically about husbands who are indeed, at least ostensibly, recognizing both the harm their sin has done and their own guilt for that sin, and requesting forgiveness for that sin. The main complication in this situation is the word *ostensibly*—meaning, the outward or apparent recognition of harm and guilt. But keep in mind, an abuser is a manipulator. Even if he is a recovering manipulator, a victim has likely spent years living in a cruel cycle of tearful regret followed eventually by more abuse.

What proves sincerity is new patterns of selfless behavior established over time in a context he no longer attempts to control, as we indicated in our answer to the previous question. This is also essential for re-establishing trust..

Trust of another person is never commanded in Scripture. The object of every command to trust in Scripture is God Himself. This doesn't mean all people are untrustworthy, only that the primary direction of our trust is God Himself, and all other trusts are derived from that. What that means is, the more a person has lived a life demonstrating responses that are like God, the more trustworthy he is.

Practically, this means you should not pressure an abused wife to trust her seemingly repentant husband. She can be willing to forgive him and even to love him without yet trusting him. Instead of focusing on her relative degree of trust in him, you should focus your care for her on two things. First, focus on the power of the gospel to change a man's heart so that his behavior changes, and these changes will be evident in time. And second, focus on the duty of the community of faith to ensure that change is permanent by both holding the repentant sinner accountable and by being vigilant to protect the grieved person. These focuses will allow the right atmosphere for trust to flourish, if the husband indeed demonstrates changed behavior over time.

How do I give wise counsel regarding reunification after abuse?

As described above, Scripture upholds a high view of marriage and forbids divorce for any reason except two: sexual immorality and spousal abandonment. In those cases, the spouse not guilty of those covenant-breaking sins is not obligated to maintain the covenant. Still, reconciliation and reunification may be possible if repentance is demonstrated as genuine over time, as described above.

But before we describe how reunification may occur, we offer this warning: Reunification must not be the *presumed solution*. Presuming it makes harm to abuse victims more likely and undermines genuine repentance in an abuser. Insisting that reunification is the solution will prevent the hard work of an actual solution from taking place. Instead, it should be considered a *possible outcome* if it proves to be in line with the whole range of biblical values.

Often the driving question in everyone's mind (except the victim) is *How long should we wait for reunification?* This question is understandable, both for a husband who wants to be home and for church leaders who want to honor the marriage covenant. But we believe this is the wrong question to ask because it makes two errors: First, it wrongly assumes reunification is the wisest, most biblical answer. Second, it implies that time is the primary consideration in determining if the features necessary for responsible reunification are in place. Reunification is not *the* goal in addressing abusive marriages, but can be *a* goal that's prioritized properly amidst other goals.

Even considering reunification after abuse requires time, patience, and vigilance. To put it simply, you should not suggest an abused wife return to the same marriage. It must be a different marriage she is returning to. By *different*, we mean that the old patterns of abuse will never again be allowed to take hold and grow in the dark. Notice how we stated this. She should not make her decision based on a presumed guarantee that abuse is no longer possible in this marriage. Rather, she should make her decision based on what demonstrable changes are now in place that make abuse unable to thrive in secret. Specifically, reunification can be responsibly considered with at least these three changes in place: (1) the ongoing effects of harm on the victim, (2) the established indicators of heart change in the abuser, and (3) the commitment of ongoing community accountability.

In terms of the ongoing effects of harm on the victim, you can help her describe how she's presently perceiving the abuse she endured and what present effects it's having on her. Does she feel strong enough to identify manipulative tactics for what they are instead of falling under their spell? Is she trusting the Lord with any lingering sense of guilt, failure, or anger? Does she understand the distinction between love and trust? Is she considering reunification out of her freedom in Christ or out of fear of embarrassment or the circumstances of being a divorced woman?

In terms of the established indicators of heart change in the abuser, we've tried to lay those out above. What we will add here, however, is vital: You need to understand *her* perception of these indicators. Your opinion, or anyone else's, is less important than hers in making this decision. What you're helping her determine is if she has confidence that change has been adequately demonstrated for the step of reunification to occur. This confidence will not be completely absent of fear, but it should not be characterized fundamentally by fear. If it is, that's indication that the needed confidence is not there.

In terms of the commitment of ongoing community accountability, the victim should have confidence that others will help protect her from any hint of abuse dynamics emerging again. At this point in the process, hopefully multiple viewpoints of accountability have been orchestrated, including family, church members, and legal authorities as needed. All of this is to prevent the self-contained environment of abuse from being allowed ever again. Again, what's important here is that *she* is confident that these external checks are in place, that they are *for* her, and that she can reach out to them any time without shame.

With these three changes in place, you can help a victim consider whether the Lord is calling her to reunification. Your job is not to make the decision for her, but to help her use the biblical principles above to consider the changes that may or may not be adequately established for such a decision.

Appendix C:

National and State Domestic Violence Resources

NATIONAL DOMESTIC VIOLENCE HOTLINE
(UNITED STATES)
800-799-SAFE (7233)
800-787-3224 TDD
www.thehotline.org
(IF IN IMMEDIATE DANGER, ALWAYS CALL 911)

The National Domestic Violence Hotline was authorized in the Violence Against Women Act, signed into law on September 13, 1994. It was established on August 17, 1995 through funding received by the Texas Council on Domestic Violence. It is headquartered in Austin, Texas, and recently added a new digital services office in Washington, DC. The Hotline® is a 24/7 national resource for shelters and service providers across the U.S.

NATIONAL DOMESTIC ABUSE HELPLINE (UNITED KINGDOM)
0808-2000-247
www.nationaldahelpline.org.uk
(IF IN IMMEDIATE DANGER IN THE UK, PLEASE CALL 999)

1800RESPECT (AUSTRALIA)
1800 737 732
www.1800respect.org.au
(IF IN IMMEDIATE DANGER IN AUSTRALIA, PLEASE CALL 000)

Global Trauma Recovery Institute
www.missio.edu/global-trauma-recovery-institute

National Coalition Against Domestic Violence
www.ncadv.org

Domestic Shelters
www.domesticshelters.org

FOCUS Ministries, Inc.
www.focusministries1.org

National Sexual Assault Hotline
1-800-656-HOPE (4673)
www.rainn.org (24 hour chat)

Teen Dating Violence Hotline
(866) 331-947 24 Hr call or text
www.LoveIsRespect.org (24 hour chat)

Victim Advocacy Training
Called to Peace Ministries
Joy Forrest, Founder and Executive Director

CTPM provides support groups, advocacy training, and church partnerships.
www.calledtopeace.org

ReStoried: A Support Group for Women
Fieldstone Counseling
Melissa Affolter, Facilitator
Provides support groups for victims.
www.fieldstonecounseling.org

Training for Perpetrator Care
PeaceWorks
Chris Moles, Founder
Provides training, coaching, a weekly podcast, and other resources for gospel-centered domestic abuse care.
www.chrismoles.org

Men of Peace Intervention Groups for Men
Provides Men of Peace groups for perpetrators.
www.menofpeace.org

State Domestic Violence Organizations

If you're looking for local resources, such as victim shelters, batterer intervention programs, or other coordinated community response agencies, we recommend starting with your state coalition or network. They will be able to direct you to resources in your locality.

The Alabama Coalition Against Domestic Violence
1420 I-85 Parkway
Montgomery, AL 36101
(334) 832-4842 Fax: (334) 832-4803
(800) 650-6522 Hotline
Website: www.acadv.org

Email: info@acadv.org

Alaska Network on Domestic Violence and Sexual Assault
130 Seward Street, Suite 214
Juneau, AK 99801
(907) 586-3650 Fax: (907) 463-4493
Website: www.andvsa.org
Email: andvsa@andvsa.org

Arizona Coalition Against Domestic Violence
2700 N. Central Avenue, Suite 1100
Phoenix, AZ 85004
(602) 279-2900 Fax: (844) 252-3094
(800) 782-6400 Nationwide
Website: www.acesdv.org
Email: info@acesdv.org

Arkansas Coalition Against Domestic Violence
700 S. Rock Street
Little Rock, AR 72202
(501) 907-5612 Fax: (501) 907-5618
(800) 269-4668 Nationwide
Website: www.domesticpeace.com
Email: info@domesticpeace.com

California Alliance Against Domestic Violence
1107 9th Street, #910
Sacramento, CA 95812
(916) 444-7163 Fax: (916) 444-7165
(800) 524-4765 Nationwide
Website: www.cpedv.org
Email: info@cpedv.org

Colorado Domestic Violence Coalition
1330 Fox Street, Suite 3

PO Box 40328
Denver, CO 80204
(303) 831-9632 Fax: (303) 832-7067
(888) 778-7091 Toll-Free
Website: www.ccadv.org
Email: info@violencefreeco.org

Connecticut Coalition Against Domestic Violence
655 Winding Brook Drive, Suite 4050
Glastonbury, CT 06033
(860) 282-7899 Fax: (860) 282-7892
(888) 774-2900 In State DV Hotline
Website: www.ctcadv.org

Delaware Coalition Against Domestic Violence
100 West 10th Street, Suite 903
Wilmington, DE 19801
(302) 658-2958 Fax: (302) 658-5049
Website: www.dcadv.org

District of Columbia Coalition Against Domestic Violence
5 Thomas Circle Northwest
Washington, DC 20005
(202) 299-1181 Fax: (202) 299-1193
Website: www.dccadv.org
Email: info@dccadv.org

Florida Department of Children and Families
ACCESS Central Mail Center
P.O. Box 1770
Ocala, FL 34478-1770
(850) 300-4323 Fax: 1 (866) 886-4342
1 (800)-500-1119 In State DV Hotline
Website: www.myflfamilies.com

Georgia Coalition on Family Violence, Inc.
114 New Street, Suite B
Decatur, GA 30030
(404) 209-0280 Fax: (404) 766-3800
(800) 334-2836 Crisis Line
Website: www.gcadv.org

Hawaii State Coalition Against Domestic Violence
1164 Bishop Street, Suite 1609
Honolulu, HI 96813
(808) 832-9316
Website: www.hscadv.org
Email: info@hscadv.org

Idaho Coalition Against Sexual and Domestic Violence
Linen Building
1402 W. Grove Street
Boise, ID 83702
(208) 384-0419
Website: www.idvsa.org
Email: info@engagingvoices.org

Illinois Coalition Against Domestic Violence
806 South College Street
Springfield, IL 62704
(217) 789-2830
(877) 863-6338 In State DV Hotline
Website: www.ilcadv.org

Indiana Coalition Against Domestic Violence
1915 West 18th Street, Suite B
Indianapolis, IN 46202
(317) 917-3685
(800) 332-7385 In State
Website:www.icadvinc.org

Iowa Coalition Against Domestic Violence
4725 Merle Hay Road, Suite 107
Urbandale, IA 50322
(515) 244-8028 Fax: (515) 244-7417
(800) 770-1650 In State Victim Hotline
Website: www.icadv.org

Kansas Coalition Against Domestic Violence
634 Southwest Harrison Street
Topeka, KS 66603
(785) 232-9784 Fax: (785) 266-1874
(866) 363 2287 In State Crisis Hotline
Website: www.kcsdv.org
Email: coalition@kcsdv.org

Kentucky Coalition Against Domestic Violence
111 Darby Shire Circle
Frankfort, KY 40601
(502) 209-5382 Phone
Website: www.kcadv.org

Louisiana Coalition Against Domestic Violence
P.O. Box 77308
Baton Rouge, LA 70879
(225) 752-1296
(888) 411-1333 Statewide DV Hotline
Website: www.lcadv.org

Maine Coalition to End Domestic Violence
One Weston Street
Augusta, ME 04330
(207) 430-8334
(866) 834-4357 Statewide DV Hotline
Website: www.mcedv.org
Email: info@MCEDV.org

Maryland Network Against Domestic Violence
4601 Presidents Drive, Suite 300
Lanham, MD 20706
(301) 429-3601 Fax: (301) 809-0422
(800) 634-3577 Statewide Helpline
Website: www.mnadv.org
Email: info@mnadv.org

Massachusetts Coalition Against Sexual Assault and Domestic Violence
745 Atlantic Avenue
8th Floor, Suite 800
Boston, MA 02111
(617) 248-0922
(877) 785-2020 SafeLink Statewide Hotline
(877) 521-2601 TTY
Website: www.janedoe.org
Email: info@janedoe.org

Michigan Coalition Against Domestic Violence
3893 Okemos Road, Suite B-2
Okemos, MI 48864
(517) 347-7000 Fax: (517) 347-1377
(517) 381-8470 TTY
Website: www.mcedsv.org
Email: general@mcedsv.org

Violence Free Minnesota
60 East Plato Blvd., Suite 230
St. Paul, MN 55107
(651) 646-6177 Fax: (651) 646-1527
Website: www.vfmn.org

Mississippi State Coalition Against Domestic Violence
P.O. Box 4703

Jackson, MS 39296
(601) 981-9196 Fax: (601) 981-2501
(800) 898-3234 State Hotline
Website: www.mcadv.org
Email: support@mcadv.org

Missouri Coalition Against Domestic and Sexual Violence
217 Oscar Drive, Suite A
Jefferson City, MO 65101
(573) 634-4161
Website: www.mocadsv.org

Montana Coalition Against Domestic Violence
P.O. Box 818
Helena, MT 59624
(406) 443-7794
(888) 404-7794 Toll Free
Website: www.mcadsv.com
Email: mtcoalition@mcadsv.com

Nebraska Coalition to End Sexual and Domestic Violence
245 S. 84th Street, Suite 200
Lincoln, NE 68510
(402) 476-6256
Website: www.nebraskacoalition.org

The Nevada Coalition to End Domestic and Sexual Violence
250 South Rock BLVD., Suite 116
Reno, NV 89502
(775) 828-1115 Fax: (775) 828-9911
Website: www.ncedsv.org

New Hampshire Coalition Against Domestic Violence
P.O. Box 353
Concord, NH 03302

(603) 224-8893 Fax: (603) 228-6096
(866) 644-3574 In State DV Hotline
Website: www.nhcadsv.org

New Jersey Coalition for Battered Women
1670 Whitehorse Hamilton Square Road
Trenton, NJ 08690
(800) 572-7233 In State DV Hotline
Website: www.njcbw.org

New Mexico Coalition Against Domestic Violence
2340 Alamo Avenue, SE, Suite 120
Albuquerque, NM 87106
(505) 246-9240
Website: www.nmcadv.org
Email: info@nmcadv.org

The New York State Coalition Against Domestic Violence
119 Washington Avenue, Suite 12210
Albany, NY 12054
(518) 482-5464 Fax: (518) 482-3807
(800) 942-5465 English-In State
(800) 942-6908 Spanish-In State
Website: www.nyscadv.org

North Carolina Coalition Against Domestic Violence
3710 University Drive, Suite 140
Durham, NC 27707
(919) 956-9124 Fax: (919) 682-1449
Website: www.nccadv.org

North Dakota Council on Abused Women's Service and Alliance to End Partner Abuse
521 E. Main Avenue, Suite 320
Bismarck, ND 58501

(701) 255-6240 Fax: (701) 255-1904
(888) 255-6240 Toll Free
Website: www.cawsnorthdakota.org

Action Ohio Coalition for Battered Women
P.O. Box 423
Worthington, OH 43085
(614) 825-0551 Fax: (614) 825-0673
(888) 622-9315 Toll Free
Website: www.actionohio.org
Email: actionohio@wowway.biz

Ohio Domestic Violence Network
1855 E. Dublin Granville Road
Columbus, OH 43229
(614) 781-9651
(800) 934-9840
Website: www.odvn.org

Oklahoma Coalition Against Domestic Violence and Sexual Assault
8524 S. Western, Suite 111
Oklahoma City, OK 73139
(405) 524-0700 Fax: (405) 524-0711
Website: www.ocadvsa.org

Oregon Coalition Against Domestic and Sexual Violence
9570 SW Barbur Boulevard, Suite 214
Portland, OR 97219
(503) 230-1951 Fax: (503) 230-1973
Website: www.ocadsv.com
Email: info@ocadsv.com

Pennsylvania Coalition Against Domestic Violence
3605 Vartan Way, Suite 101

Harrisburg, PA 17110
(717) 545-6400
Website: www.pcadv.org

Rhode Island Coalition Against Domestic Violence
422 Post Road, Suite 102
Warwick, RI 02888
(401) 467-9940 Fax: (401) 467-9943
(800) 494-8100 In State
Website: www.ricadv.org
Email: ricadv@ricadv.org

South Carolina Coalition Against Domestic Violence and Sexual Assault
P.O. Box 7776
Columbia, SC 29202
(803) 256-2900 Fax: (803) 661-7327
Website: www.sccadvasa.org
Email: info@sccadvasa.org

South Dakota Coalition Against Domestic Violence and Sexual Assault
122 East Sioux Avenue, Suite D
Pierre, SD 57501
(605) 945-0869 Fax: (605) 945-0870
(800) 572-9196 Nationwide
Website: www.sdcedsv.org

Tennessee Task Force Against Domestic Violence
2 International Plaza Drive, Suite 425
Nashville, TN 37217
(615) 386-9406
(800) 356-6767 State DV Hotline
Website: www.tncoalition.org

Texas Council on Family Violence
P.O. Box 163865
Austin, TX 78716
(512) 794-1133 Fax: (512) 685-6397
(800) 525-1978 Toll Free
Website: www.tcfv.org
Email: info@tcfv.org

Utah Domestic Violence Advisory Council
124 South 400 East, Suite 430
Salt Lake City, UT 84111
(801) 521-5544 Fax: (801) 521-5548
(800) 897-5465 24 hour LINK line
Website: www.udvc.org
Email: admin@udvc.org

Vermont Network Against Domestic Violence and Sexual Assault
P.O. Box 405
Montpelier, VT 05601
(802) 223-1302 Fax: (802) 223-6943
(800) 228-7395 Statewide DV Hotline
Website: www.vtnetwork.org

Virginians Against Domestic Violence
1118 West Main Street
Richmond, VA 23230
(800) 838-8238 24 Hour Domestic and Sexual Violence Hotline
Website: www.vsdvalliance.org
Email: info@vsdvalliance.org

Washington State Coalition Against Domestic Violence
Olympia Office
711 Capitol Way South, Suite 207

Olympia, WA 98501

Seattle Office
1511 Third Avenue, Suite 433
Seattle, WA 98101
(206) 389-2515 Fax: (206) 389-2520
Website: www.wscadv.org
Email: wscadv@wscadv.org
'In Her Shoes' Training Resource for Adults (see website)
'In Their Shoes' Training Resource for Teens (see website)

Washington State Native American Coalition Against Domestic and Sexual Assault (Women Spirit Coalition)
542 North 5th Avenue, Suite C
Sequim, WA 98382
(360) 681-3710 Fax: (360) 681-3745
Website: www.womenspirit.net

West Virginia Coalition Against Domestic Violence
5004 Elk River Road South
Elkview, WV 25071
(304) 965-3552 Fax: (877) 335-2306
Website: www.wvcadv.org

End Domestic Abuse Wisconsin: The Wisconsin Coalition Against Domestic Violence
1400 East Washington Avenue, Suite 227
Madison, WI 53703
(608) 255-0539
Website: www.endabusewi.org

Wyoming Coalition Against Domestic Violence and Sexual Assault
P.O. Box 236
710 Garfield Street, Suite 218

Laramie, WY 82073
(307) 755-5481 Fax: (307) 755-5482
(844) 264-8080 Toll-Free
Website: www.wyomingdvsa.org
Email: info@wyomingdvsa.org

U.S. Virgin Islands

Family Resource Center in St. Thomas
2317 Commandant Gade
Charlotte Amalie, St Thomas 00802
(340)-776-3966 Fax: (340)-776-5994
(340)-776-7867 National Hotline
Website: www.usvifrc.org
Email:frcdevelopment@gmail.com

Women's Coalition of St. Croix
45 Fisher Street
Christiansted, Virgin Islands 00820
(340) 773-9272 (24/7 Hotline and Main Number)
Fax: (340) 773-9062
Website: www.wcstx.org
Email: info@wcstx.org

Puerto Rico

Oficina De La Procuradora De Las Mujeres
161 Juan Ponce de León Avenue
San Juan, 009 17
(787) 721-7676 Fax: (787) 721-7711
1-877-722-2977 Toll Free
(787) 725-5921 TTY
Website: www.mujer.pr.gov

Elder Care

The Eldercare Locator
(800) 677-1116
eldercare.acl.gov (online chat and email available)

The National Center on Elder Abuse
c/o University of Southern California Keck School of Medicine
Department of Family Medicine and Geriatrics
1000 South Fremont Avenue, Unit 22, Building A-6
Alhambra, CA 91803
(855) 500-3537
Website: ncea.acl.gov
Email: ncea-info@aoa.hhs.gov

National Committee for the Prevention of Elder Abuse
Website: preventelderabuse.org

Nursing Home Abuse Center
101 S New York Ave Suite 201
Winter Park, FL 32789
(800) 478-0520
nursinghomeabusecenter.com

AARP/Legal Counsel for the Elderly
601 E Street NW
Washington, DC 20049
(202) 434-2120
Website: www.aarp.org/legal-counsel-for-elderly/

American Bar Association

Commission on Law and Aging
1050 Connecticut Ave. NW, Suite 400
Washington, DC 20036
(202) 662-8690 Fax: (202) 662-8698

Website: www.americanbar.org/aging
Email: aging@americanbar.org

Children

Resource Center on Domestic Violence: Child Protection and Custody
1-800-527-3223
Website:www.rcdvcpc.org
Email: info@rcdvcpc.org

National Council on Child Abuse and Family Violence
P.O. Box 5222
Arlington, VA 22205
(202) 429-6695
(703) 567-6706
Website: preventfamilyviolence.org
Email: nccafv@aol.com or info@nccafv.org

Appendix D:

A Sample Church Domestic Abuse Policy

Our church has created this domestic abuse policy to protect intimate partners, children, and others residing in the homes of our church members and attenders when domestic abuse occurs within those homes.

Abuse occurs as a person in a position of greater influence uses his personal capacities to diminish the personal capacities of those under his influence in order to control them. Because God made people as embodied souls, these personal capacities are both physical and spiritual. Abuse is identified from two directions: (1) the manipulative intent and behavioral forcefulness of the one in a position of influence, and (2) the diminishing effect on those under his influence.

- Abuse is an assault upon the image of God in another human being.

- Abuse usually occurs in a pattern that is typically increasing in frequency and/or intensity.

- Abuse is intentional, though the abuser may not be self-aware enough to recognize the intentions of his or her heart. Abuse is never perpetrated by accident.

- Abuse is about the misuse of power to control or manipulate another for selfish gain. It is an act of oppression.

- Abuse can involve physical, emotional, verbal, sexual, economic, spiritual, or psychological means. Sadly, the abuse is often perpetrated through a combination of these.

- The goal of abuse is self-gratification—to get what one wants at the expense of another.

Domestic violence in any form—physical, sexual, emotional, economic, psychological or spiritual—is an assault upon the image of God in a fellow human being, and is therefore an assault upon God Himself. When it is between a husband and a wife, it further violates the one-flesh covenantal relationship that God established. Under no circumstance is abuse ever justified. Neither is it ever the fault of the victim. Domestic abuse severely damages relationships and often destroys the relationship beyond repair. An act of abuse is never an act of Christian love. Christ's self-giving love encourages the flourishing of the individual, while domestic abuse seeks to limit the victim's capacities through dominance, replacing love with fear. Given this acknowledgement, the elders of Our Church affirm the following:

- Domestic abuse in all its forms is sinful and incompatible with the Christian faith and a Christian way of living.

- All abuse is spiritually damaging for both the victim and the abuser, and has collateral damage that extends to children, extended family, and close friendships.

- Domestic abuse is a serious problem which occurs in church families as well as in wider society.

- Domestic abuse is not primarily an anger problem, a marriage problem, the victim's problem, or even simply a legal problem, but rather a sin problem.

- Statistically, domestic abuse is primarily perpetrated by men, against the very people whom God has given these men to protect and shepherd—women and children.

- We will listen to, take seriously, support, and care for those affected by domestic abuse.

- We will urge abused persons to consider their own safety and that of family members first and to seek help from the church, professional counseling, and legal resources, to bring healing to the individuals and, if possible, to the marriage relationship.

- We will not seek to investigate charges of abuse, but will refer both the abused person and the perpetrator of the abuse to competent professional counselors, and potentially legal counsel, and rely upon their determinations.

- We will not encourage marriage counseling in cases of domestic abuse until both parties and their counselors are in agreement that they are ready for marriage counseling.

- We will report suspected abuse of children, the elderly, and the disabled to the proper authorities without delay, in accordance with the laws of our state.

- We will call abusers to repent and wait patiently for them to demonstrate consistent fruit of repentance before acknowledging repentance.

- We will discipline abusers and remove them from the church if they are unrepentant.

- We will work with local domestic violence support agencies, will learn from them and support them in appropriate ways.

- We will teach that domestic abuse is a sin.

- We will teach what it means to be male and female image-bearers of God, equal in value, dignity and worth.

- We will train all pastors, elders, deacons, and lay leaders in an appropriate domestic abuse awareness and response training, and update this training regularly.

- We will seek to utilize trained professionals to encourage best practices and keep church members and leadership trained on and informed about the implementation of this domestic abuse policy.

Appendix E:

A Sample Role Description For a Domestic Abuse Care Advocate

Role: Care Advocate. A Care Advocate is one of a group of people trained to provide specialized support and accountability for someone who has been a victim or perpetrator of domestic abuse. Our first priority is the safety and support of the victim and children. Our hope is to help the church bring care to victims and correction to perpetrators so that both can be reconciled to the Lord and (if possible) to each other, for the glory of God.

Care Advocates may be mobilized in one of the following ways:

- Assigned to an individual identified as a perpetrator or victim of abuse as the main point person representing the church in coordinating care and providing accountability for a specific season of time.

* Compassionate care for a member/attender identified as a victim of abuse.

* Loving confrontation for a member/attender identified as a perpetrator of abuse.

* Communicating with the victim as needed regarding interactions and the process.

* Communicating to the perpetrator regarding corrective care in the church.

* Average time commitment: 2 hours a week to the assigned member/attender.

- Lead or co-lead a support group for victims or an education/accountability group for perpetrators.[1]

Limitations of Role. Care advocacy does NOT include:

- Direct or professional-level counseling
- Mediation between spouses
- Directives on divorce or separation
- Legal advice or directives

Requirements.

- Church member in good standing

---

1. We recommend the following resources if your church is interested in implementing support groups for domestic abuse. For support of victims, Joy Forrest's Called to Peace Ministries (https://www.calledtopeace.org) offers online support groups. Mending the Soul (https://mendingthesoul.org) provides group materials as well as facilitator materials and training for facilitators. Diane Langberg has also authored a curriculum (book and workbook) for survivors of sexual abuse, titled *On the Threshold of Hope*. For education/accountability for perpetrators, Chris Moles (http://www.chrismoles.org) provides the *Men of Peace* coaching groups for perpetrators and the *Men of Peace* curriculum (https://www.menofpeace.org), and provides training for Men of Peace facilitators and perpetrator care advocates through his PeaceWorks University.

- Already serving in lay or staff leadership, with current and clear background check
- Full alignment with the ministry objectives of Our Church's care ministry
- Caring, compassionate heart for both victims and perpetrators of abuse
- Courage to provide accountability to a perpetrator of abuse, and/or support to a victim in a potentially dangerous situation
- Prompt and clear communication
- Teachable
- Completion in good standing of a church-approved training program on caring for victims and correcting perpetrators.[2]

Responsibilities.

- Handle details regarding the victim with extreme discretion.
- Place the safety and support of the victim as the highest priority.
- Communicate regularly with designated church leadership contact regarding all communication and actions taken with assigned victim/perpetrator.
- Communicate weekly (or other arranged scheduled) with your assigned victim/perpetrator to provide support and accountability.
- Coordinate with church leadership contact and others as needed to provide resources that might be helpful for the victim's/perpetrator's recovery.

---

2. For training in caring for victims, we recommend Joy Forrest's Called to Peace Ministries (https://www.calledtopeace.org) care advocacy training. For training in correction of perpetrators, we recommend Chris Moles' (http://www.chrismoles.org) PeaceWorks University.

- Participate in care meetings as necessary for training, support, and encouragement.

Appendix F:

When Wives Abuse Husbands

In this appendix, we will attempt to apply the framework of discerning abuse dynamics that we laid out in Chapter 3 to domestic violence by women against men. To be clear: this section is *not* intended to allow room in your mind for a category of 'mutual abuse,' where both parties are at fault because a wife is abusive to her husband too.[1] Rather, this section is intended

---

1. Given our complementarian position, we believe that when both spouses are acting abusively, the male as the designed initiator and head of the home holds primary responsibility, in part because of the greater potential to cause harm, and should be addressed accordingly. If a husband who has been confronted about his abusive treatment of his wife uses the ideas outlined in this appendix to mitigate his responsibility in any way for his own abusive behavior, he is demonstrating the very manipulative tendencies that are part of abuse. True repentance and change occur as the focus is own personal responsibility.

to acknowledge that abuse can occur in the direction of wife to husband. The following is intended to help you respond with wisdom and compassion in situations where a husband innocent of abuse himself approaches you to disclose that he is being abused.

Women as much as men can be corrupted in their perception, leading to abusive interactions. They can use their strengths—physical, relational, intellectual—to weaken or diminish their husbands, causing lasting effects on him. Such situations require the same compassionate involvement we are encouraging for female victims, even though they are less common by reason of design. These situations also require awareness of the unique dynamics that may be in play—such as the stigma and shame associated with being a male victim and the potential incredulity of their community.

When helping in a domestic abuse situation involving a male victim by a female abuser, you can use the same basic steps outlined in this book. But we also want to recognize a few distinct aspects of this experience that may help you care wisely for adult male victims.

- **Abuse can occur when a wife uses her superior capacities to diminish her husband's personal capacities in order to control him.**

   Some people may find it hard to believe that a woman can abuse a man because their conception of abuse doesn't extend beyond physical assault, and the average woman is able to inflict less damage on a man than a man can on a woman. But a more thorough understanding of abuse allows more insight here.

   Physical abuse can involve something other than assault. A woman may not be able to overpower a man, but she can certainly create conditions that diminish his ability to feel physically safe. She can break objects, throw them at him, or use them as weapons. She can slap or hit him repeatedly or unexpectedly. She can lock him out of, or in places. In sum, she can condition him to fear physical harm if he does not comply.

But abuse can also occur in non-physical ways. A wife can threaten, disparage, or rage at her husband in ways that have lasting effect on his ability to think outside the world those words create. She can react with violent emotions, threaten self-harm or harm to children, threaten to end the marriage or expose him to public ridicule. A wife can establish a long pattern of coercion and control over her husband that has a diminishing effect on his personhood.

- **Male abuse victims will likely be operating out of their own warped perception and behavior in response to their abuse.**

  As with female abuse victims, male abuse victims will likely not see the world rightly as a result of the abuse they've endured. This leads to a diminished ability to act rightly in response.

  The longer or more severe the abuse is, the more they will have a hard time seeing their marriage, themselves, and even God rightly. They will likely blame themselves, feel that they couldn't possibly reach out for help, or think that God is unable to help them in their situation. They may imagine that no one else would possibly understand, so they're on their own.

  This warped perception will likely display itself in warped behavior—mainly, ways of coping with their pain that are not honoring to the Lord or good for them. Often the key to them is passivity. They may avoid addressing the problem by fleeing to any number of other refuges—from alcohol and drugs to amusements and hobbies, from work to ministry. They build up a pattern of avoidance.

- **Male abuse victims may struggle with a sense of failure, emasculation, and shame.**

  An abused husband may struggle with a unique form of shame that comes from a mixture of biblical and unbiblical ideas about marriage, masculinity, and God. He may feel a mix of proper guilt for wrong decisions or poor leadership *and* an improper guilt for assuming that his sins make him deserve the abuse he's receiving. He may simply be relegating himself to being a failed man who simply needs to endure what his life has become.

  If an abused husband is distressed enough to disclose this to you (not as a defensive tactic avoiding responsibility for his abuse), you should receive him with the same compassion. Be aware that his tendency may be to passively resign himself to the situation he's in, even later isolating from the people he's disclosed to in shame.

- **Male abuse victims will need their own advocacy in the church community.**

  Many uncharitable things may be said of a man who is abused by his wife. He will likely be very sensitive to this fact. You should assure him early and often that you will walk with him through the process of protecting him, addressing the abuse in his marriage, and shepherding the people of the church to respond rightly. You can remind him of the distinction between short-term and long-term considerations. The question of what needs to be publicly known is not a short-term issue. The immediate concern is his safety and the safety of any children involved. You can commit that when the time comes to consider how the church will respond, you will help everyone think biblically and compassionately.

The issues involved in situations where husbands are abused by their wives deserves far more attention than this appendix provides. Our main intention in this book is to address wives as the overwhelming majority of victims. But we hope this brief appendix allows you to have eyes to see the distress that abused husbands may face.

Also available from Christian Focus Publications...

Eryl Davies

HIDDEN EVIL

A Biblical & Pastoral Response
To Domestic Abuse

Hidden Evil

A Biblical and Pastoral Response to Domestic Abuse

D. Eryl Davies

Domestic abuse is an ugly, but all too real, problem that is often not dealt with well within our churches. Eryl Davies tells the stories of domestic abuse survivors – both men and women – who have been let down by their churches' reactions. How are we to respond biblically to such situations? How do pastors and church leaders address this problem when both victim and abuser are part of their congregation? As well as making the reader aware of the reality of this issue, Davies gives helpful guidelines and suggestions for church leaders dealing with cases of domestic abuse.

… a must-read for all in church leadership, especially in Bible-believing churches, and perhaps particularly in independent churches. It should also be read by as many Bible-believing Christians as possible.

Hector Morrison
Principal, Highland Theological College, Dingwall

ISBN 978-1-5271-0331-3

A Certain Brightness

Bible Devotions for Troubled Times

Philippa Ruth Wilson

A Certain Brightness

Bible Devotions for Troubled Times

Philippa Ruth Wilson

The devotions in this book are short, encouraging, and a reminder of the light when everything seems dark. Philippa Wilson has begun each chapter with a five-word Bible phrase that is easily memorised and ended with a prayer. Beautiful illustrations by Rebekah Lesan make this an ideal book to give to friends who are struggling.

This is a lovely book. Pastoral, sensitive and full of wisdom, it offers comfort and companionship to those who are struggling. I've been blessed and encouraged by it. I am thankful to Philippa for sharing from her own experiences and for reminding me of the God who shines brightest in the dark.

Emma Scrivener
Blogger at emmascrivener.net and author of *A New Name* and
A New Day

These simple, yet profound, devotions, bring the light and life of scripture to those who are struggling through times of darkness and depression. Philippa writes with raw honesty, gentle humour and, above all, Christ—centred hope. There are treasures here for all of us, however we are feeling.

Vaughan Roberts
Rector of St Ebbe's, Oxford and Director of Proclamation Trust

ISBN 978-1-5271-0691-8

THE
CREAKING
ON THE
STAIRS

FINDING FAITH IN GOD
THROUGH CHILDHOOD ABUSE

MEZ McCONNELL

The Creaking on the Stairs

Finding Faith in God Through Childhood Abuse

Mez McConnell

I think there is real hope to be found, in the middle of our deepest traumas, in the good news about Jesus Christ. I also think that there is a place for us to find hope and community within the church. Because of these two beliefs, I truly think, distant though it may be, that we may even get to a place of peace within our souls and a place of forgiveness for those who hurt us so much.

This is a book that has no easy answers and will offer none. This is a book that tries to get behind the tough questions of why God permits such abuses to occur in this world. Using his own story of childhood abuse, Mez McConnell tells us about a God who is just, sovereign and loving. A good father who knows the pain of rejection and abuse, who hates evil, who can bring hope even in the darkest place.

It's not a pagan rags to Christian riches story. It's real, raw and radical. I suspect that there will be as many people shocked by the Bible teaching that Mez wrestles with, as there will be those shocked by the abuse he suffered. With chapters like 'The glorious, wonderful reality of Hell' and 'The terrible reality of Heaven', there is no chance of this book being perceived as comfortable.

David Robertson
Pastor and apologist

ISBN 978-1-5271-0441-9

Christian Focus Publications

Our mission statement –

STAYING FAITHFUL

In dependence upon God we seek to impact the world through literature faithful to His infallible Word, the Bible. Our aim is to ensure that the Lord Jesus Christ is presented as the only hope to obtain forgiveness of sin, live a useful life and look forward to heaven with Him.

Our books are published in four imprints:

CHRISTIAN FOCUS

Popular works including biographies, commentaries, basic doctrine and Christian living.

CHRISTIAN HERITAGE

Books representing some of the best material from the rich heritage of the church.

MENTOR

Books written at a level suitable for Bible College and seminary students, pastors, and other serious readers. The imprint includes commentaries, doctrinal studies, examination of current issues and church history.

CF4•K

Children's books for quality Bible teaching and for all age groups: Sunday school curriculum, puzzle and activity books; personal and family devotional titles, biographies and inspirational stories – because you are never too young to know Jesus!

Christian Focus Publications Ltd,
Geanies House, Fearn, Ross-shire,
IV20 1TW, Scotland, United Kingdom.
www.christianfocus.com